Mohan Trivedi

Heuristic Reasoning about Uncertainty:
An Artificial Intelligence Approach

Paul R. Cohen
Department of Computer and Information Science,
University of Massachusetts at Amherst

Heuristic Reasoning about Uncertainty: An Artificial Intelligence Approach

Pitman Advanced Publishing Program
BOSTON · LONDON · MELBOURNE

PITMAN PUBLISHING LIMITED
128 Long Acre, London WC2E 9AN

PITMAN PUBLISHING INC
1020 Plain Street, Marshfield, Massachusetts 02050

Associated Companies
Pitman Publishing Pty Ltd, Melbourne
Pitman Publishing New Zealand Ltd, Wellington
Copp Clark Pitman, Toronto

First published 1985

Dedication
To **Carole Ruth Beal**, for everything

British Library Cataloguing in Publication Data

Cohen, Paul R.
Heuristic reasoning about uncertainty: an artificial intelligence approach.—(Research notes in artificial intelligence. 2)
1. Artificial intelligence 2. Problem solving
3. Uncertainty 4. Heuristic programming
I. Title II. Series
001.53′9 Q335

ISBN 0-273-08667-7

Library of Congress Cataloging in Publication Data

Cohen, Paul R.
Heuristic reasoning about uncertainty.
Bibliography: p.
1. Uncertainty (Information theory) 2. Heuristic programming. 3. Artificial intelligence. 4. SOLOMON (Computer program) I. Title.
Q375.C64 1985 001.53′9 84-25533

ISBN 0-273-08667-7

Reproduced and printed by photolithography
in Great Britain by Biddles Ltd, Guildford

Contents

Acknowledgements

This work has been shaped by many individuals. Some have helped with the rough hewing, and others with the fine points. To all, I wish to express my deep gratitude.

My friend and companion Danny Asher suggested portfolio management as a domain for this work. I was then fortunate to meet Mark D. Lieberman, of Drexel Burnham Lambert, who agreed to be the domain expert for the FOLIO program, and was avid and thoughtful thoughout. The FOLIO effort continued over a year, without complaint from Mark, who was told initially that it would take a few weeks. Professor William F. Sharpe, of the Graduate School of Business at Stanford University, helped me with FOLIO´s mathematical algorithms, taught me much about portfolio management and investment, and later agreed to serve on my reading committee. I am very grateful for his insights and enthusiasm for FOLIO and the model of endorsement.

My thanks to the members of my committee, Douglas B. Lenat (Chair), William F. Sharpe, Edward H. Shortliffe, and Amos Tversky. Four academic departments are represented by this committee, and it is due to the efforts of the committee that the work in this dissertation is of general relevance. I wish to thank Doug Lenat, a fountain of ideas, for his enthusiasm and advocacy. Ted Shortliffe invariably and immediately focussed on the weak points of the model of endorsement. I am grateful to him for making the model -- and this document -- very much stronger by his incisive and perceptive comments, and for his help with the probabilistic end of things. Amos Tversky has cheerfully raised numerous, difficult, and subtle questions. My thanks to him for providing research questions for years to come, and for his encouragement about the potential of this work.

The model of endorsement was developed in a series of conversations with Milton R. Grinberg, of Stanford University. Our collaboration was spirited, productive, and a high point of my stay at Stanford. It has been my good fortune to find in Milt a critic, a colleague, and a friend.

I would also like to thank Avron Barr, Gary Bonitatibus, Tom Dietterich, and Anne Gardner for their thoughtful comments about the developing model of endorsement, and for their camaraderie and kindness during our years at Stanford, especially during the exciting years of the *Handbook of Artificial Intelligence*. I have a great debt to the technical editor of the *Handbook*, Dianne Kanerva, who taught me to write quickly and without fear. This skill, learned during two years of close collaboration, is invaluable, and my gratitude to Dianne for her patient tutelage and friendship is inestimable.

I have a special debt to Professor Edward A. Feigenbaum. He invited me to Stanford to work for just a year on the first volume of the *Handbook of Artificial Intelligence*. Instead, I stayed for five years, through *three* volumes, co-editing the third with Ed. I owe much of what I have, and of what I have done, to Ed's kindness and generosity.

I have been fortunate, in the year since this document was first printed, to have found excellent colleagues at the University of Massachusetts at Amherst. They have helped much with the development of the theory of endorsements. I wish to acknowledge the contributions of Norm Carver, Alvah Davis, David Day, Brian Delaney, Tom Gruber, Philip Johnson, Larry Lefkowitz, Melinda Mesick, and Mike Sullivan.

This research was funded by a grant from NL Industries, for which I am grateful.

My debts to my colleagues are great, but I owe no-one as much as I owe Carole R. Beal. I expect it will take a lifetime to repay her.

1 Introduction

1.1 The Problem

The problem addressed by this document is how to represent and reason with heuristic knowledge about uncertainty. We know much about uncertain situations besides our *degree* or strength of belief: We discriminate among many *kinds* of uncertainty, and we know many approaches to resolving or discounting uncertainty. We recognize different kinds of evidence, we prefer some kinds to others, and we recognize that our certainty depends not only on evidence but also on the *importance* of the uncertain situation. We can judge the "utility" of evidence, and decide whether it is worth the effort to obtain it. Remarkably, in a world where almost nothing is certain, we use our knowledge about uncertainty to behave *as if* almost nothing is uncertain. How can we represent and reason with this all-important knowledge about uncertainty? This document proposes an artificial intelligence approach -- a model of heuristic reasoning about uncertainty implemented as a computer program.

Uncertainty is not a new problem to academic research. Indeed, its has been studied in great depth by decision analysts, statisticians, philosophers, psychologists, gamblers, insurance companies, as well as practitioners of artificial intelligence (AI). One might legitimately question the utility of more research on uncertainty. The approach to uncertainty of this research is novel in a number of respects: Uncertainty is represented in terms of its effects on reasoning; it is viewed as a structured object that traverses a line of reasoning, an object whose properties change with the style of reasoning, and with the availability, type, and quality of evidence. Particular kinds of uncertainty, when they interfere with problem solving goals, are themselves regarded as problems to be solved. Part of the proposed model of reasoning about uncertainty concerns how these "uncertainty problems" are resolved or discounted. Although this research concentrates on aspects of the model that enhance the reasoning abilities of AI programs, the superordinate goal of the research is to develop a plausible model of human reasoning about uncertain situations. Clearly, to the extent that this goal is achieved, the relevance of this work goes beyond artificial intelligence.

Artificial intelligence is a fortuitous discipline from which to study reasoning about uncertainty. The AI approach regards reasoning as composed of interacting information processes, and as active and constructive. AI methods encourage one to view uncertainty as a problem to be solved by the application of heuristic knowledge. Given this perspective, it is natural to study the *effects* of uncertainty on reasoning processes. For example, to solve a problem, we first state goals, then think about an order in which to achieve them, then search for methods to achieve the goals, and so on. Consider the effects of uncertainty on the process of ordering goals: If the goals are disjunctive, such that solving any one solves the entire problem, then our first attempts should be to solve the goals for which we have the best evidence; but if the goals are conjunctive, such that *all* must be solved, then we should first attempt the goals for which we have the *poorest* evidence, because if these attempts fail, we can save ourselves the effort of working on the other goals. Even this rudimentary reasoning about uncertainty and evidence can obviously have profound effects on the efficiency of problem solving. But it depends on a sufficient representation of knowledge about uncertainty: For the example to succeed, we must represent the strength of evidence for and against each of the goals, and whether the goals are conjunctive or disjunctive. These are simple requirements, easily achieved with current AI technology.

But AI lacks the tools to manage other kinds of knowledge about uncertainty. The previous example was managable because the logical structure of goals (i.e., whether they are conjunctive or disjunctive) is usually explicit in the statement of the goals, and because strength of evidence is easily represented by numbers. But in other cases "strength of evidence" is actually a summary of several factors that pertain to certainty, and if an intelligent reasoner normally discriminates among these factors, then the summary representation is inadequate. For example, you may be equally certain that there are no Venusians and that the Palo Alto municipal swimming pool is not painted green and pink. You believe there are no Venusians because there is no evidence of Venusians, but the conclusion is not entirely certain because if there *were* Venusians, you would not necessarily know about them. You believe that the Palo Alto municipal swimming pool is not green and pink because you have never seen any such swimming pool, but you are not entirely certain because you have never seen the Palo Alto pool. Thus the strength of belief of each statement is composed of a reason to believe and a reason to disbelieve. The difference between the statements is that the nonexistence of Venusians is unprovable (at least in the short run) while the coloration of the Palo Alto municipal pool is demonstrably not pink and green. This difference is not captured in the strengths of belief of the statements, and it is not even necessarily important if we limit our reasoning to assessing evidence for and against the statements. But, if we intend to use the statements in subsequent arguments, then the ability to discriminate among provable and unprovable statements becomes useful. For example, we may decide to limit our reasoning entirely to statements that are disprovable, on the grounds that non-disprovable statements -- however credible -- reduce the credibility of the arguments they support. This kind of reasoning exceeds the capabilities of current formal approaches to reasoning under uncertainty.

The reasoning of the previous example is qualitatively different, for several reasons, from common numerical approaches to uncertainty in AI and other disciplines. First, the emphasis is on decomposing strengths of belief into reasons for believing and disbelieving. Second, these reasons are not blindly tallied, as strengths of belief often are, but are subject to heuristic reasoning; for example, we may survey our statements of evidence and decide to use non-disprovable statements only if none of our evidence is disprovable. Thus, the weight of all evidence is not calculated in the same way, but depends on the kind of evidence, on the immediate and ultimate problem-solving goals, on the standards one applies to judge arguments, and so on. Third, given *reasons* to believe and disbelieve statements, their *strength* of belief may become irrelevant; for example, evidence that cannot be disconfirmed is less preferable *regardless* of its credibility. These differences lead me to the term "reasoning *about* uncertainty," in preference to the more frequently used "reasoning *under* uncertainty"; my intention is to emphasize that uncertainty is itself an object of reason.

To reiterate, the problem addressed by this research is to represent and reason with the knowledge we have about uncertainty. As the previous paragraphs suggest, the appropriate course is to develop a representation suitable to expressing reasons for believing and disbelieving, and to specify the effects of these reasons on problem-solving processes -- on intelligent reasoning.

1.2 The SOLOMON Program

This document describes an artificial intelligence approach to uncertainty called the *model of endorsement* and the structure of a program -- called SOLOMON -- that implements the model. Endorsements are the structured objects that represent reasons for believing and disbelieving the propositions with which they are associated. SOLOMON uses endorsements to control its reasoning about uncertainty and evidence. Reasons for believing are called *positive* endorsements, reasons for disbelieving, *negative* endorsements. The program uses a modified backward-chaining control structure to prove statements in the predicate calculus. Currently, SOLOMON is a "toy" system that works with just a few inference rules, endorsements, and other kinds of knowledge. It is intended ultimately as a tool for building rule-based expert systems in domains where reasoning about uncertainty is necessary.

The following example illustrates some of the central ideas in the model of endorsement and SOLOMON:

> Consider the question of which of several cars to buy. Test-driving cars is time-consuming and unpleasant, so we want to limit our search to a few likely cars. We search for evidence about numerous cars by posting a bulletin on an electronic bulletin board, asking for information about the candidate manufacturers and models. We get two kinds of responses from drivers who are either satisfied or dissatisfied with their cars. This "evidence" for or against each kind of car has one of two endorsements: Responses from people who *own* the cars they describe get the **long-term** endorsement; and responses from people who comment on cars that they rented, borrowed, or otherwise drove for just a short time, get the **short-term** endorsement. We decide that, for the purpose of *eliminating* cars from consideration, either endorsement is adequate. This is tantamount to saying that a brief but inadequate experience with a car is as compelling evidence as a long and inadequate experience, at least for the purpose of eliminating a car from consideration. Thus, any car that gets a poor review is eliminated. This leaves half a dozen cars that get good reviews. To further narrow the field, we decide to eliminate any recommendation endorsed as **short-term**, on the grounds that a brief affair with a car does not provide the opportunity to observe its subtle strengths or weaknesses. This still leaves two contenders, so we decide to test drive both of them.

One thing to note about the example is that the endorsements, **short-term** and **long-term**, are not general comments about any evidence, but are specific reasons to disbelieve and believe evidence about things that people own, such as cars. It is assumed here that any domain will have a characteristic set of endorsements. However, in an attempt to build a general system, the SOLOMON program works with a small set of very general endorsements.

A second observation is that the *adequacy* of evidence depends on what one intends to use it for. For the purpose of eliminating cars from consideration, evidence endorsed as **short-term** is considered adequate; but for the purpose of including cars in the candidate list, it is considered inadequate. Note that domain knowledge is required to decide in which contexts an endorsement is adequate. The

SOLOMON program uses rules to decide when evidence is "believable enough," and this decision depends on the endorsements of the evidence and on the purpose to which the evidence will be put.

The example also suggests that endorsements can be ranked, at least in the default sense that adequately endorsed evidence is *more believable* than evidence that is inadequately endorsed. Beyond this, SOLOMON also has general rules for ranking adequately endorsed pieces of evidence, although this poses considerable difficulty when evidence is supported by combinations of endorsements (but see Section 5.5). Domain knowledge is required, of course, to rank domain-specific endorsements.

Finally, note that when the available evidence does not support a choice between two options, it is possible to *resolve* the conflict in other ways. The example ends with two options that are equally believable (i.e., they are both supported by evidence endorsed as **long-term**). The question of which car to test-drive cannot be resolved on the basis of the available evidence, but it can be resolved by driving both cars. Methods to resolve uncertainty are domain-dependent: The general "do both" strategy for resolving conflicts may work for test-driving cars, but it is an expensive resolution for conflicts about which car to *buy*. SOLOMON has knowledge about which general resolution methods are appropriate for which kinds of uncertainty.

In sum, this example illustrates four kinds of knowledge that are required in the model of endorsement to reason about uncertainty. These are endorsements, criteria for when endorsements qualify a statement as certain enough to use as evidence, criteria for ranking endorsements, and rules for generating resolution tasks. (An important kind of knowledge that was not illustrated in the simple example concerns how endorsements propagate over inferences.) Individual problem domains are assumed to afford characteristic kinds of endorsements, as well as the criteria for reasoning with them. SOLOMON, however, is an attempt to capture some fairly general endorsements and reasoning methods. This is partly because of difficulties in obtaining endorsements of inference rules in SOLOMON's test domain, and partly because of a desire to develop a general tool for building expert systems.

1.2.1 Why SOLOMON?

SOLOMON's namesake, King Solomon, was very famous for his wisdom, and so one is hesitant to use his name for an AI program. However, the choice is not inappropriate. A tale of Solomon's wisdom is found in First Kings, Chapter 3: Solomon was approached by two harlots, each of whom claimed to be the mother of a baby. The one argued that her child was stolen by the other, whose own child had died in the night. The scriptures go to lengths to show how little evidence Solomon had to work with; for example, one harlot says "there was no stranger with us in the house, save we two in the house." In other words, there were no witnesses; the king had to judge based on two pieces of equally plausible, conflicting testimony. His solution was to order the child cut in two. When one woman protested, less grieved to relinquish the child than to see it chopped up, the king recognized her as the true mother.

Possibly, this story will seem unrelated to the theory of uncertainty in AI but, in fact, it illustrates three basic precepts of the model of endorsement. First, reasoning about uncertainty requires knowledge, and lots of it. Solomon knew much more than the harlots told him; he used commonsense knowledge to fill in the details, to recognize conflict as a source of uncertainty; and he used wisdom to resolve the conflict by evoking more evidence. Second, the choice of a method to resolve or discount uncertainty depends on explicit representation of the reason for uncertainty. In Solomon's case, the reason was conflicting testimony, and the resolution method was to force the situation to some extreme point where the two women would no longer make identical claims. Other kinds of uncertainty succumb to other methods, provided the type of uncertainty is made explicit. Third, it is imperative to record one´s motives for acting, if one is to justify one´s decisions later. It is quite possible that Solomon ordered the baby chopped in half because he thought it would be equitable, or because he was irritated by the whole situation. The uncertainty about Solomon´s motives no doubt provides good fare for hermeneutics, but reasoning about uncertain situations should not itself introduce uncertainty -- by shoddy record-keeping -- if it can be avoided.

1.3 Normative and Performance Approaches to Uncertainty

Uncertainty is most often represented in terms of probability. It is natural to speak of the probability of life on Venus or the odds that a football team will win a match. Moreover, probability theory provides a relatively simple calculus for adjusting probabilities in the light of evidence. Once probability is accepted as an appropriate representation of uncertainty, it becomes possible to contrast human performance under uncertainty with performance as specified by probability theory. Descriptions of the first kind are called *performance* or *positive* theories, and theories of reasoning that are consistent with the axioms of probability theory are called *normative*. Human reasoning under uncertainty is clearly not normative (e.g., Edwards, 1968); even expert reasoning violates results from probability theory (e.g., Eddy, 1982; Tversky and Kahneman, 1971). Much has been learned about human judgment and decision by comparing it with normative models. The models serve as a basis for comparison and thus for a vocabulary of effects: Conservatism is conservatism with respect to the outcome of a normative analysis. Systematic deviations from normative models are seen as evidence of *heuristics* in human reasoning about uncertainty.[1]

There are disciplines in which non-normative reasoning is undesirable, for example, calculating odds in poker or blackjack. (The term *prescriptive* is sometimes used for normative theories because they specify what one *should* do if, for example, one wants to play poker or blackjack as well as possible.) Other disciplines, such as cognitive psychology, welcome non-normative behavior as an object of study. There is some question about the attitudes of researchers in artificial intelligence. It has long been recognized in AI that heuristic reasoning is a source of power, that the model of humans as perfect processors of information is not only inaccurate but is also unlikely to lead to efficient and intelligent reasoning. Aspects of cognition that at one time were regarded as "bugs," now appear to be "features"; for example, limited short-term memory serves an important purpose in focusing attention, and is now mimicked by the *agenda* mechanism and other control processes. It is therefore puzzling that AI retains models of reasoning under uncertainty that are derived from normative theories, the more so because the assumptions of the normative approaches are frequently violated, and because the probabilistic interpretation -- and numerical representation -- of uncertainty summarizes and fails to discriminate among reasons for believing and disbelieving. One may speculate that AI uses quasi-probabilistic, numerical methods for reasoning under uncertainty less for any advantages of normative reasoning than for lack of other methods. The research described in this document is an attempt to develop a new method that has obvious advantages over the old.

Two questions that must be asked of a new approach to reasoning about uncertainty are whether the approach is normative and, if so, what does

---

[1] The main spokesmen for this view were and are Kahneman and Tversky, and their colleagues (see, e.g., Tversky and Kahneman, 1974; Kahneman and Tversky, 1979; Tversky and Kahneman, 1981. See also Kahneman, Slovic, and Tversky for a wide-ranging collection of papers on judgment.)

"normative" mean? No attempt has been made to represent uncertainty in terms of probability, and so if the model described here is normative, it clearly is not in the sense of conforming to the axioms of probability theory. But there is a prescriptive component to this research: It is that one should keep all available knowledge about uncertainty explicit. We shall see later that human and artificial reasoning must violate this prescription for the sake of efficiency, and that human systematic deviations from this property might be just as interesting to a model of human reasoning about uncertainty as deviations from the axioms of probability theory. (It is worth noting that "normative" probabilistic approaches to uncertainty violate the prescription, except in the cases where the only knowledge one has of an uncertain outcome is its probability.)

1.4 Evaluating the Research

What are the criteria for success if one's goal is to develop a new approach to uncertainty? Past research in AI, particularly vision research and expert systems research, provides some guidelines. In vision work, a novel idea is initially implemented in a clumsy, ad hoc, heuristic computer program. The program undergoes refinements, but remains heuristic. Then, the idea is analysed by someone with mathematical training, and the dozens of heuristics that made the system run are replaced with a mathematical theory of, say, obtaining surface orientation from intensity gradients. There is a progression from heuristic reasoning to reasoning with a theory. In expert systems research, there is no expectation that heuristic reasoning will give way to an underlying theory; indeed, the power of expert systems derives not from any formal characterization of a domain but from the numerous tricks of the trade developed by experts in years of practice. In expert systems research there is a progression from poorer to better representational and reasoning tools. The approach to uncertainty developed in this document should be evaluated as a tool for representing and reasoning about uncertainty, that is, by the criteria that are applied to tools in expert systems research. But the progression that characterizes vision research -- from ad hoc programs to their underlying theory -- should also apply to heuristic knowledge about uncertainty. Eventually, after the initial, ad hoc, heuristic attempts reported here, one may expect a formal theory of this knowledge.

Initial criteria for success, however, will be utilitarian. Is the approach natural, or does it violate intuitions about uncertainty and evidence? What aspects of uncertainty are especially easy or difficult to express? What kinds of tasks are especially amenable to this approach, and why? Does the approach depend on unrealistic assumptions about the user and the accuracy of information? Does it produce answers that people find unacceptable? The overriding question is, will people use the results of this research? We defer the question of whether using this approach violates theoretical principles such as consistency, parsimony, and the axioms of probability theory.

1.5 A Guide for the Reader

This document is divided into three large chapters and one smaller one. The second, third, and fourth chapters are intended as a progression of arguments for the model of endorsement -- the main contribution of this research. Chapter 2 surveys current approaches to uncertainty and introduces the model of endorsement, Chapter 3 presents comparisons between the model and probabilistic approaches to uncertainty, and Chapter 4 discusses an implementation of the model in a computer program. The goal of this organization is to nudge numerical approaches out of their preeminent position in AI by stages. By the end of Chapter 4 one should understand the alternative approach, its assets and limitations, and one should believe that the approach works. Chapter 5, which discusses problems for future research, may dampen one´s enthusiasm for the model of endorsement, since much work remains to be done. But this seems inevitable, given the novelty of the approach.

The second chapter -- Managing Uncertainty -- describes several approaches to uncertainty in AI. The two general approaches that have been most productive are that of associating *parallel certainty inferences* -- calculations of how much one believes -- with domain inferences; and the approach of designing a control structure to exploit some aspect of the task environment, such as redundancy, to minimize uncertainty. The second part of the chapter (section 2.3) outlines the model of endorsement, which is the main theoretical contribution of this research. Section 2.3.5 relates the model of endorsement to other work in AI and cognitive science.

Chapter 3 is intended to "place" the model of endorsement among other approaches to reasoning about uncertainty. To this end, two lengthy, parallel analyses of arguments are presented. In each case, one analysis is by probabilistic methods and the other by the model of endorsement. The first analysis is of a static "evidence-weighing" problem; here the goal is to decide which of several hypotheses is most believable. This kind of task does not circumscribe all that we mean by reasoning under uncertainty: After evidence is weighed, decisions are made, and conclusions are used as evidence in subsequent evidence-weighing tasks. In general, statements function both as evidence and as conclusions. The second analysis in Chapter 3 extends the first to the account for the dual role of statements.

Following these preparatory chapters, Chapter 4 describes the SOLOMON program, which is an implementation of the model of endorsement. The reader who wants a quick introduction to the research without many details might read sections 2.3 and 4.2. The chapter on SOLOMON covers design goals, representation of knowledge, endorsers and endorsements, SOLOMON´s control structure, and three examples of SOLOMON at work.

Chapter 5 describes the contributions of the model of endorsement and the state of the SOLOMON program, and proposes a number of improvements to the program. The endorsement-based approach to reasoning about uncertainty is novel, and this document leaves a number of questions unanswered or incompletely answered. These questions and the applicability of the model of endorsement to current AI problems are described in this chapter. The last section of the chapter is a brief synopsis of my work since this document was first published in the form of a technical report.

2 Managing Uncertainty

2.1 Introduction

The purpose of this chapter is to review a number of techniques from different disciplines for dealing with uncertainty. The first section of this chapter is a general discussion of approaches to uncertainty as they have been adopted for use in AI programs. Four general approaches are discussed. The *engineering* approach is to remove uncertainty from the task domain, that is, to define or constrain one's task in such a way as to avoid representing and reasoning about its inherent uncertainty. Next we will briefly consider the *diversification* heuristic. Diversification is presented as a method for *discounting* uncertainty, particularly uncertainty about future events. A third class of techniques involves *parallel certainty inferences*. When an inference is uncertain, it can be augmented by another whose purpose is to calculate the certainty of the first. This approach is represented by three subsections on Bayesian theory, the Dempster-Shafer theory, and the theory of fuzzy sets. A final perspective on uncertainty in AI is the *control* approach, typified by programs such as HEARSAY-II, which manage uncertainty with control structures that exploit redundancy or some other aspect of the task domain.

The second section of the chapter introduces the model of endorsement. The purpose of the model is to provide us with a representation and calculus for reasoning with structured symbolic information about uncertainty. The structures are called *endorsements*. Two analogies to reasoning about endorsements are discussed. In the first, an endorser is viewed as a bureaucrat whose job is to ensure that some task or proposal satisfies particular requirements. In fact, endorsers attach endorsements -- reasons for believing or disbelieving -- to propositions. Since endorsers' requirements pertain to the certainty of a proposition, the endorsement of a particularly stringent endorser is equivalent to a high degree of confidence in the proposition. When several tasks have each accrued several endorsements, one might ask which task is the most believable. The analogy that illuminates this question is that of a ledger book. Evidence for and against a proposition is arranged in the *pro* and *con* columns of the ledger book, respectively. It turns out that one´s total belief in the proposition cannot be had by summing up the *con* evidence and subtracting it from the *pro* evidence, or any other simple operation, because pieces of evidence are not equally believable. Thus, the *accounting* in the ledger book analogy depends on the endorsements of the pieces of evidence.

After a brief introduction to endorsements, I will review some work in AI and cognitive science that pertains to the idea.

The orientation of this chapter and the next is towards the representational, adequacy and utility of the various approaches to uncertainty. Normative and performance criteria are not much discussed. My orientation is identical with that of Shafer and Tversky (1983) in their discussions of Bayesian and belief function theories:

> We do not focus here on the question of whether these theories are accurate descriptions of how people think. We ask instead whether people are capable of using the theories and whether they can use them to given ends -- whether, for example, they can use them to formalize and refine certain intuitively reasonable patterns of thought. Nor do we address here the question of whether the theories are "normative" -- it seems premature to prescribe the use of a given tool before we have an adequate understanding of how well and to what ends it can be used. Furthermore, the prescriptions can only be given relative to a given set of alternative tools and to a usually ill-defined set of problems. (Shafer and Tversky, 1983, p. 8)

The criteria for discussing and comparing the model of endorsement with other approaches to uncertainty are just the kinds of questions that AI practitioners ask of developing representational languages (Barr and Feigenbaum, 1981, Chapter 3): What aspects of uncertain situations are especially easy or difficult to represent, and can one represent all pertinent aspects of uncertainty? How much expertise is needed to use the representation; is there a lengthy phase of decomposing and reorganizing one's arguments about evidence and uncertainty? Does the representation make unrealistic assumptions about the accuracy of the information it requires from a user? How explicit is the reasoning of the user in the final representation of his or her assessements? Does the technique scale up from individual problems to sequences of inferences? And so on.

What is the point of developing a new representation and calculus for uncertainty, when probability seems to have served so well for so long? It is a commonplace in AI that any representation language favors some kinds of concepts at the expense of others. Thus, one should not expect the language of endorsements to adequately represent all aspects of all uncertain situations, but one should expect it to facilitate the expression of concepts that were previously difficult to express. It follows that endorsements are not proposed as a complete *replacement* for probabilistic and other approaches to uncertainty. Since different representations of uncertainty facilitate expressions about different kinds of uncertain situations, the development of new representations naturally expands our understanding of uncertainty. For example, the theory of fuzzy sets was a response to *vagueness*, a characteristic of many of the terms we use in science and everyday language. The theory has increased our understanding of vagueness. Finally, with each new representation, it becomes more clear that theories of probability, possibility, endorsements, and so on, are just tools to help us express and reason about uncertain situations.

2.2 The Representation and Management of Uncertainty in AI Programs

2.2.1 The Engineering Approach

The engineering approach to uncertainty is simply to formulate one´s problem to avoid explicit representation of and reasoning with uncertainty. One first recognizes that the kind of uncertainty that arises is intractable given current techniques, and then one decides how to avoid it. For example, in AI research on legal reasoning one might expect a theory of uncertainty in evidence, but, in fact, there is none, partly because the kind of uncertainty implicit in legal reasoning is beyond the representational tools current in AI:

> When hard legal questions do arise, their basis is quite different from the sources of uncertainty usually described in connection with expert systems. They do not generally involve insufficient data, for example, or incomplete understanding of the workings of some physical process. Instead, an especially important source of hard questions is the open texture of legal predicates -- that is, the inherent indeterminacy of meaning in the words by which fact situations are classified into instances and noninstances of legal concepts. (Gardner, 1983).

In this kind of situation, a degree of ingenuity is required to engineer uncertainty out of the task domain. Gardner (1983), for example, works on bar-exam problems in which the evidence is presumed to be accurate and believable.

Most AI programs engineer uncertainty out of the task domain to some extent. Any program that accepts a description of the world rather than constructing it -- as do vision and speech understanding programs -- from raw sensory data has had problems of noise and ambiguity removed. This is necessary to progress. Sometimes, however, the degree of abstraction from the real world is so great that one wonders whether the new problem has any correspondence to the original. For example, the BACON program (Langley, 1980) discovers physical laws such as Kepler´s law from observations. However, the observations are not "observed" but are carefully constructed and ordered to facilitate discovery. Moreover, the observations are assumed to be accurate:

> BACON is unable to handle noisy training instances. The triggering of constancy detectors, for example, is based on the near equality of the values seen in as few as *two* training instances. Such calculations are highly sensitive to noise. (Dietterich, 1982)

Obviously, Bacon's contemporaries were not treated to such carefully prepared and noise-free (guaranteed!) data, Langley's claim that BACON is a model of "Baconian science" notwithstanding.

One potential problem with engineering uncertainty out of one's task domain is that, in doing so, one may lose a valuable source of constraints. This is especially the case when we are uncertain about how to use available information, and so we simply ignore it. The information may, in fact, have useful characteristics. An example of this occurred in early scene analysis research, where it was assumed that shadows complicated scenes, making them harder to understand. Accordingly, scenes were given even and uniform illumination, and all shadows were eliminated. David Waltz (1972) showed that shadows were, in fact, an important source of information, although it was necessary to develop an algorithm to exploit their constraints.

Another source of uncertainty that is often engineered out of the task domain is the question of whether data are *relevant*. This is especially the case for learning programs (Dietterich, 1982; Michalski, Carbonell, and Mitchell, 1983), where training cases may be preclassified into relevant instances and noninstances of a concept. Alternatively, instances may not be preclassified, but feedback is given to allow the learning program to develop its own classification. In this case, it is difficult for a system to learn without some assurance that the training instances are relevant (i.e., not noise).

Assumptions of relevance are discussed in the context of logical systems by McCarthy (1980). He proposes the *circumscription* mechanism that allows one to assume that only explicitly mentioned factors are relevant to a problem (see also section 4.4.1.1 and Doyle, 1982). A similar kind of assumption is needed to tackle the *frame problem* (McCarthy and Hayes, 1969). This problem involves uncertainty about the side effects of an action: If I engage in some problem solving action, such as moving a chess piece from one square to another, there is uncertainty about all the ramifications of the move, just as there is uncertainty about which ramifications are relevant to my goals. It is common to make the so-called *STRIPS* assumption -- named for the STRIPS program (Fikes, Hart, and Nilsson, 1972) -- that the only relevant effects of an action are those that are explicitly noted.

Related to the STRIPS assumption is the *closed world assumption* which is used to delimit what a system must know (Reiter, 1980). The closed world assumption says "If *x* is true, then I would know *x* is true." Thus, it allows one to conclude that something is not true if one does not know that it is true. This assumption is very useful in engineering uncertainty out of problems, because without it, lack of knowledge of the truth of a proposition would result in lingering uncertainty about the proposition. The assumption is discussed in more detail in Chapter 4 section 4.4.1.1.

In summary, most AI practitioners engineer some uncertainty out of their programs' task domains. Three examples are assuming noise-free data, assuming relevant data, and making some delimiting assumptions about what one knows. It is worth noting that these examples all use *assumption* as a method to resolve the uncertainty associated with *incomplete knowledge*. This is a particularly problematic kind of uncertainty for AI systems, not just because AI systems know less than humans, but also because the classic modes of inference followed by such systems can lead to a kind of paralysis:

> A robot with common sense would begin an automobile trip by walking to the place where it expects the car to be, rather than sitting immobilized, thinking about the infinite variety of ways in which circumstances may have conspired for it not to be there. From a formal point of view, there is no way to prove that it is still there, but nevertheless one must act, and must do so on the basis of plausible assumptions. (Winograd, 1980, p. 6)

One problem with assumptions is that they may have to be retracted later. So-called *non-monotonic logics* have been developed to cope with the problems of maintaining consistency that arise from the possibility of retraction (see, for example, the April, 1980 issue of *Artificial Intelligence*).

Besides the difficulties associated with non-monotonic inferences, there is the more mundane danger that by overzealous limiting of uncertainty one can develop a program that corresponds only slightly to the original task for which it was designed. Also, we face the problem that some information for which we lack processing algorithms may, in fact, be a useful source of constraints.

2.2.2 Diversification

Diversification is a method for discounting uncertainty. It is a fascinating process in which one trades something one wants for certainty. For example, at the horse races one can bet everything on one horse or divide one´s assets and bet on all the horses in a race. The latter strategy involves diversification: One has traded away a desirable but uncertain result -- picking the winner or an exacta combination – for the certainty that *one* of the several bets will pay off. This strategy takes the fun out of a day at the races, but is entirely appropriate for situations where uncertainty is not fun, such as selecting drugs in medical diagnosis or investing money for risk-averse clients. These are two domains in which diversification has been used in AI. In MYCIN (Shortliffe, 1974), it often happened that a consultation resulted in not one but a small group of diagnoses;

that is, MYCIN was not completely certain which of two or more bacteria actually afflicted a patient. MYCIN's strategy was to find the smallest number of best-recommended drugs that covered for all candidate diagnoses. Since drugs have side-effects, this is a classic diversification strategy, in which MYCIN traded away something desirable (few side-effects) for certainty that the disease was covered for, whatever its identity.[1] A second, more implicit, case of diversification is found in the FOLIO system (see Cohen and Lieberman, 1983). FOLIO builds portfolios with a goal-programming algorithm, a form of linear programming that minimizes the deviations from desired levels of multiple goals. It sometimes happens that uncertainty about clients' needs and wants result in conflicting goals, such as "maximize capital gains income" and "minimize risk to principal." In these cases, the uncertainty is resolved essentially by diversification – by the goal programming algorithm that attempts to satisfy both goals.

Diversification seems to be an appropriate strategy for discounting uncertainty about alternatives whenever one lacks the evidence to choose one alternative, and when no more evidence is forthcoming. Whenever there is no act, request, or experiment that will increase one's certainty, diversification seems to be the optimal strategy. Thus, it is especially useful for uncertainty about future events (see also the discussion of least commitment planning in section 2.2.7 of this chapter.)

2.2.3 Parallel Certainty Inferences: Introduction

The parallel certainty inference approach is probably the most popular in AI, and is what is commonly thought of as reasoning under uncertainty. At its most general, the technique splits reasoning in uncertain domains into two more or less dependent processes. In the first, conclusions are derived as if under certainty. In

[1] The trade was not entirely side-effects for an increased ***probability*** of covering for the disease, since utility considerations also entered into the swap. Efforts were made to cover for particularly dangerous disease even if their probablility was low.

the second process, the goal is to decide *how much* the conclusions of the first process are to be believed. This decomposition of reasoning under uncertainty into two processes makes sense, especially if the processes are largely independent. As a rule, one´s strength of belief in conclusions has easily controlled effects on the process of deriving conclusions. (For exemplary discussions of this approach in AI systems, see Shortliffe and Buchanan, 1975; Duda, Hart, and Nilsson, 1976; Szolovits and Pauker, 1978; Shortliffe, Buchanan, and Feigenbaum, 1979; Duda, Gaschnig, and Hart, 1979; Quinlan, 1982).

Parallel certainty inferences are typically numerical inferences. But there is no reason in principle why this should be so. The purpose of these inferences is to tell one how much to believe or disbelieve the conclusions with which they are associated. This does not preclude symbolic reasoning about one´s reasons for believing and disbelieving. Indeed, the model developed in this document adopts the parallel certainty inference model, and the objects it propagates over inferences are not numbers but reasons for belief.

The goal in parallel certainty inference systems is to determine which states of the world are most likely to hold. For example, MYCIN tries to identify the bacteria that most likely account for a patient´s signs and symptoms; and in PROSPECTOR (Duda, et al., 1979) the goal is to identify the likelihood that a geologic area contains particular kinds of ore deposits. Utility considerations about the virulence of a bacteria or the economic value of ore deposits are implicit in the probabilistic analyses (see section 2.2.4). Thus, the approach differs from decision-analytic techniques (Schlaifer, 1969; Hillier and Lieberman, 1980) that seek to maximize one´s *expected utility* given an unknown state of the world. Decision analysis provides an important set of tools for reasoning about uncertainty; for example, one can evaluate the worth of evidence and the utility of obtaining more evidence. But the single factor that limits the usefulness of these techniques is that they assume known utilities for the uncertain states of the world. This is an unreasonable requirement for many AI decision problems, and so it is more usual to embrace the weaker goal of finding the most likely of several alternatives, instead of the stronger goal of finding the alternative that maximizes expected utility (but see Shortliffe et al., 1979, for a review of decision-analytic techniques in clinical decision making.) Decision analysis is not one of the parallel certainty inference approaches discussed in this chapter, partly because of the requirement of expressing utilities for states of the world, but primarily because the calculation of expected utility is just an embellishment on the more basic problem of establishing the *probabilities* of states of the world. This problem is discussed in detail in sections 2.2.4 and 2.2.5.

This section will concentrate on parallel certainty inferences in *rule-based* inference systems (see, for example, Buchanan and Duda, 1982). Systems such as EMYCIN (van Melle, 1980) associate *certainty factors* with the conclusions of inference rules. A rule of the form "*IF A and B and C, THEN D*" asserts D when A, B, and C are certain; additionally, a number may be associated with D to indicate one's belief that D follows from A, B, and C. It may be that A, B, and C, though certain, suggest but do not confirm D, in which case the number associated with D might be less than the 1.0 that usually represents certainty in such systems. If A, B, or C are uncertain, then the number associated with D is modified to account for the uncertainty of its premises. These numbers are given different names by different authors; here, I will use the cumbersome but neutral term *degrees of belief* (Shafer, 1976).

A useful, though not entirely accurate, identification is between inference rules and statements of conditional probability: The premise of a rule can be thought of as evidence for (or against) the conclusion of the rule, and the degree of belief associated with the rule can be thought of in terms of the conditional probability of the conclusion given the evidence.

Numerical degrees of belief in current AI systems are of two kinds: those specified *initially* as qualifications of domain inference rules and those that are *derived* from the initial numbers as the system reasons. Initial numbers are usually supplied by domain experts; for example, an expert investment counselor may associate a *degree of belief* of 0.6 with the inference that advanced age implies low risk tolerance. It is not always clear what the 0.6 means. It may mean that 60% of the distribution of the elderly people in a sample have low risk tolerance. More often, the 0.6 represents an expert's degree of belief that a person has low risk tolerance if he or she is old. The number is presumably a summary of the reasons for believing and disbelieving the inference. Once summarized and associated with the inference rule, however, these reasons are inaccessible, at least to a computer program that uses the rules and degrees of belief.

The second kind of numerical degrees of belief are those derived as an AI system reasons. Two general operations are updating the degree of belief in a hypothesis to reflect some new evidence, and updating the degree of belief of a conclusion to reflect uncertainty about its premises. The first of these involves *pooling* evidence. One often finds several pieces of evidence for and against a hypothesis, and one wants to compute a net strength of belief in the hypothesis given all the evidence. Bayes' theorem, discussed in section 2.2.4, provides a tool for pooling evidence. It is used to calculate the conditional probability of a hypothesis given a body of evidence. The use of Bayes' theorem to combine evidence in rule-based inference systems depends on using the initial degrees of belief associated with inference rules to calculate the initial conditional probabilities that Bayes' theorem requires. This technique is discussed by Shortliffe and Buchanan (1975), and Adams, (1976), but is not presented here because it involves a restrictive assumption not normally made in Bayesian analyses.[2] A more usual Bayesian updating scheme is discussed in section 2.2.4.

[2] As we shall see in the next section, Bayesian inference often makes the assumption of *conditional independence* of evidence in a hypothesis. The technique for transforming a degree of belief in a rule into a parameter for Bayes' theorem requires also a stronger assumption of *strict independence* of evidence.

The Bayesian approach allows one to compute a degree of belief in an uncertain hypothesis *given* evidence pro and con the hypothesis. It does not tolerate uncertainty in the evidence itself; we cannot say, "Tell me how much to believe H given that we *may* have evidence for H." Yet it is often the case in AI programs, where the conclusion of one inference rule acts as the premise for another rule, that the evidence for a conclusion – its premise – is uncertain. A general schematic of the process of *propagating* degrees of belief over inferences is shown in Figure 2-1. At the top of the figure are two crude representations of domain inferences from portfolio management: Rule 1 states that advanced age implies low risk tolerance, and rule 2 infers that the client needs a high proportion of bonds if he (or she) has low risk tolerance. Associated with each rule is an initial degree of belief (0.6 and 0.8, respectively) supplied by the domain expert. These numbers are combined with the degrees of belief of their rule´s premises to produce a derived degree of belief in the conclusion. For example, if it is *certain* that risk tolerance is low, then 0.8 represents the undiluted degree of belief in the conclusion that the client should have a preponderance of bonds. But if – as in Figure 2-1 – it is less than certain that risk tolerance is low, then the degree of belief in the conclusion about bonds should be less than 0.8. In Figure 2-1, this premise is not fully believed and the certainty in the conclusion is represented by the product of 0.8 and 0.6. This technique for adjusting the certainty of a conclusion to reflect uncertainty in its premises was developed for the MYCIN program (Shortliffe, 1974), and is used in an example in section 3.4.1.

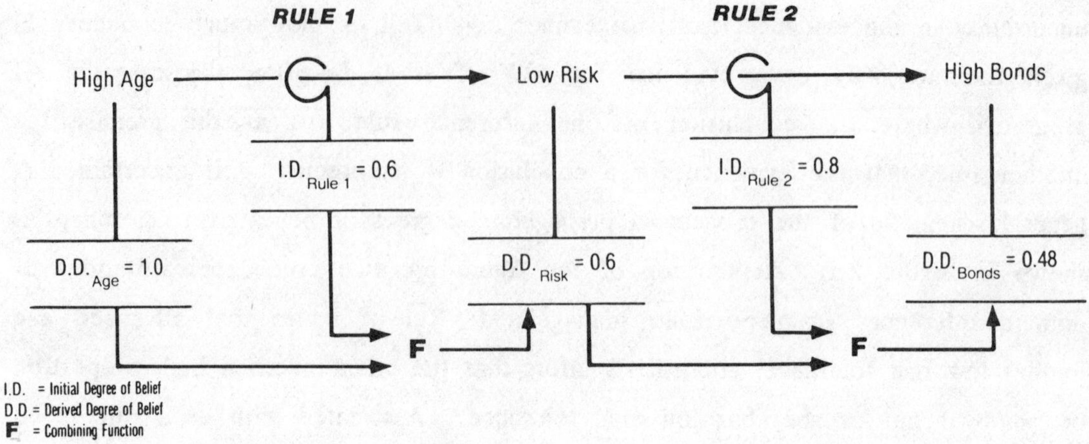

Figure 2-1: A derivation of degrees of belief

A degree of belief in a conclusion may be derived by Bayesian updating in the light of one or more pieces of evidence; or, if a conclusion is part of a chain of inferences, by an ad hoc procedure to reflect uncertainty in the premise of the conclusion. In either case, the functions that adjust degrees of belief are called *combining functions* (Shortliffe, 1974). Here we will distinguish between *pooling* combining functions, designed to pool evidence for a single hypothesis; and *propagating* combining functions, designed to propagate uncertainty about a conclusion over inferences. In a sense, inferences are made in the *context* of the degrees of belief in their preconditions, and propagating combining functions make the initial degrees of belief, associated with each inference, sensitive to these contexts. The word "context" is intended to convey the idea that situations arise dynamically that affect one´s certainty. Later it is proposed that the definition of context can profitably be broadened to include more than just the degrees of belief of preconditions.

The next three sections discuss *pooling* combining functions of various kinds, that is, they discuss how a net weight for multiple pieces of evidence for and against a hypothesis can be computed. The approaches discussed are Bayesian inference, the Shafer-Dempster theory of belief functions, and the logic of fuzzy sets. The approaches differ in the kinds of uncertainty they represent, and in their calculi for weighing evidence.

2.2.4 Bayesian Inference and Related Methods

Bayes´ theorem provides a simple mathematical method for updating the probability of a hypothesis given an observation of evidence. Thus, it is especially attractive to those who build models of diagnosis (e.g., Shortliffe, 1974) since the probabilities of current diagnoses can be easily updated as diagnostic data become available.[3] One of the problems with Bayesian updating of probabilities is that it can require huge amounts of data. Assumptions are often made to limit this requirement. In this section we develop a Bayesian updating scheme from the definition of conditional probability, identifying assumptions as they are introduced.

One often wants to know the probability of a hypothesis given some evidence. For example, one wants to know the probability that the price of Data General stock will increase given news that Data General will be involved in a merger. The parameter we desire is called the *conditional probability* that the stock price will increase, because it is the probability of an increase *in the event* that a merger is announced. If **increase** denotes the event of a stock price increase and **merger** denotes the event that a merger is announced, then P(**increase** | **merger**) denotes the conditional probability of a price increase given an announced merger.

The conditional probability of a hypothesis given some evidence is simply

---

[3] I mean diagnosis in a general "twenty-questions" sense, and include any system that uses sequentially obtained evidence to decide which of several hypotheses to believe.

$$P(h \mid e) = \frac{P(h \cap e)}{P(e)} \tag{2.1}$$

similarly

$$P(e \mid h) = \frac{P(h \cap e)}{P(h)} \tag{2.2}$$

and so

$$P(e \mid h)P(h) = P(h \mid e)P(e) = P(h \cap e)$$

from which we derive one form of Bayes´ theorem:

$$P(h \mid e) = \frac{P(e \mid h)P(h)}{P(e)} \tag{2.3}$$

Thus, if we know the *prior probability*, P(h), that the price of a stock will rise; the *likelihood*, $P(e \mid h)$, of an announced merger given a rise in the price of a stock; and the probability of one´s evidence, P(e); then we can calculate the *posterior probability*, $P(h \mid e)$, of a rise in the price of a stock given an announcement of a merger. Thus, it is straighforward to revise the prior probability of a hypothesis in the light of one piece of evidence.

This form of Bayes´ theorem is adequate if there is only one hypothesis to deal with, and if one can find P(e), but it is more usual to have several competing hypotheses. Equation (2.3) is easily extended to this case. Note first that the denominator of (2.3) can be written in terms of the conditional probabilities of e given h and $\neg h$:

$$P(e) = P(h \cap e) + P(\neg h \cap e)$$

or, from eq (2.1)

$$P(e) = P(e \mid h)P(h) + P(e \mid \neg h)P(\neg h) \tag{2.4}$$

Then, a common form of Bayes´ theorem is:

$$P(h \mid e) = \frac{P(e \mid h)P(h)}{P(e \mid h)P(h) + P(e \mid \neg h)P(\neg h)} \tag{2.5}$$

That is, eq (2.5) is written for the simple case in which h and ¬h are the only known hypotheses. This can be generalized to the case where h_i is one of n hypotheses:

$$P(h_i \mid e) \quad = \quad \frac{P(e \mid h_i)P(h_i)}{\Sigma_{j=1 \text{ to } n} P(h_j)P(e \mid h_j)} \tag{2.6}$$

Note that the identity $P(e) = \Sigma_{j=1 \text{ to } n} P(h_j)P(e \mid h_j)$ involves the assumption that the n hypotheses h_j are mutually exclusive and exhaustive, just as h and ¬h were mutually exclusive and exhaustive in (2.4).

The next extension to Bayes´ theorem is to pool several pieces of evidence for a hypothesis, instead of the single piece of evidence, e, of the previous formulations. Equation (2.6) is easily rewritten for two or more pieces of evidence:

$$P(h_i \mid e_1\& \ldots \&e_m) \quad = \quad \frac{P(e_1\& \ldots \&e_m \mid h_i)P(h_i)}{\Sigma_{j=1 \text{ to } n} P(h_j)P(e_1\& \ldots \&e_m \mid h_j)} \tag{2.7}$$

But a difficult pragmatic problem arises if we try to use this equation to combine an arbitrary number of pieces of evidence in favor of a hypothesis. The denominator of the equation implies that we need to know the conditional probabilities of all possible combinations of evidence for all possible hypotheses. This requirement is unworkable for many applications of Bayes´ theorem. To reduce the information burden, an assumption of *conditional independence* is often made. Formally, this is

$$P(e_i\&e_j \mid h) \quad = \quad P(e_i \mid h)P(e_j \mid h)$$

In words, if h is the true state of the world, then the observation of evidence e_i is independent of the observation of evidence e_j. This assumption reduces the information demand[4] of eq (2.7) and allows us to write:

$$P(h_i \mid e_1 \& \ldots \& e_m) = \frac{P(e_1 \mid h_i) \times \ldots \times P(e_m \mid h_i) \times P(h_i)}{\Sigma_{j=1 \text{ to } n} P(h_j) \times P(e_1 \mid h_j) \times \ldots \times P(e_m \mid h_j)} \quad (2.8)$$

This is the form of Bayes´ theorem that is often used to revise the probability of one of a number of exhaustive hypotheses by *pooling* the weights of pieces of evidence. We have seen that it is derived from the definition of conditional probability, and that it involves three assumptions: The hypotheses h_i are mutually exclusive and exhaustive, and there is conditional independence of the evidence in the hypotheses.

Problems with the Bayesian approach. The model presented above has a firm basis in probability theory. However, evidence is accumulating in the AI literature that this property, though desirable, is not enough to ensure that the the Bayesian scheme is adequate to the task of reasoning about uncertainty. One problem is that the assumptions involved in deriving a Bayesian combining function – mutually exclusive and exhaustive hypotheses and conditional independence of evidence in a hypothesis – do not always hold. In fact, some authors suggest that the conditional independence assumption almost never holds in their domains. Szolovits and Pauker (1978, p. 121) claim that "The assumption of conditional independence is usually false." On the other hand, this proclaimation may be overly pessimistic. In MYCIN, for example, attempts were made to structure the knowledge base in such a way as to remove dependencies between inference rules:

> Just as Bayesians who use their theory wisely must insist that events be chosen so that they are independent (unless the requisite conditional probabilities are known), we must insist that dependent

[4] Szolovits and Pauker, 1978, show that for a simple problem with 10 hypotheses and 5 binary tests as evidence, the conditional independence assumption reduces the number of conditional probabilities required for the denominator of Bayes´ theorem from 2420 to 100.

> pieces of evidence be grouped into single rather than multiple rules. (Shortliffe and Buchanan, 1975, p. 372.)

The conditional independence assumption is not the only theoretical problem associated with the Bayesian approach. A brief tour of other difficulties includes the problem that the Bayesian view of probability does not allow one to distinguish uncertainty from ignorance.[5] That is, one cannot tell whether a degree of belief was directly calculated from evidence, or indirectly inferred from an absence of evidence (but see the next section for an alternative approach.) A related problem is that the single degree of belief is a point estimate, and we know nothing about its precision. An assessed degree of belief of .5, might mean that the probability of an event is exactly .5. Alternatively it might mean that the odds of the event occurring are somewhere between 4/6 and 6/4. Another problem is that single degrees of belief combine reasons for believing with reasons for disbelieving, when one might want them kept separate. This problem was solved in MYCIN by maintaining separate measures of belief and disbelief (Shortliffe and Buchanan, 1975).

These are theoretical problems with the Bayesian scheme, but I would prefer to concentrate on pragmatic issues here. Despite inevitable inconsistencies in its rulebase, dependencies between rules, and, presumably, inaccurate and inconsistent degrees of belief assessed from its experts, MYCIN is an excellent diagnostician,

---

[5] Imagine we have three closed, opaque containers, one of which contains a diamond. Suppose we obtain evidence that suggests that container 2 holds the diamond, P(2) = .6. Ideally we would like to say only that the probability that one of the other containers holds the diamond is .4, since we have no idea of the probabilities that it is in container 1 or container 3. We have evidence of strength .4 that one of these alternatives is true, but we are ignorant beyond that. The Bayesian scheme requires probabilities for these alternatives, however, so we are forced to make a division and say, for example, that the probability distribution for the diamond is P(1) = .2, P(2) = .6, P(3) = .2. (This example suggests that the prior probability distribution is uniform; priors can be used to divide the probability 1- .6 = .4 between P(1) and P(3), thus avoiding an arbitrary assignment.) The value of .6 is based on evidence, but the values of .2 are not. Thus the Bayesian scheme confounds ignorance and uncertainty in a degree of belief.

and so are many other programs beset by similar theoretical problems. Indeed, Clancey and Cooper ran a fascinating study of MYCIN's *certainty factors* (CFs) in which they showed that "the rules use CFs that can be modified by ±.2" without seriously affecting its advice. (Buchanan and Shortliffe, 1984, Ch. 10). This result brings to mind a question raised by Davis:

> If the systems build around these mechanisms are too sensitive to the numbers produced, that's bad because no one is ready to defend the precise numbers. Yet if the systems are relatively insensitive to the numbers then all of that mechanism appears spurious. (Davis, 1979, p. 1102)

Imagine, as an extreme example, that MYCIN showed *no* decrement of performance when all CF's were rounded to either 0, .5, or 1.0. If the system works at this point, why bother with the CF mechanism? This is a pragmatic, rather than theoretical, issue. The question is not so grand as whether the CF mechanism is a normative theory of reasoning under uncertainty, but rather, whether the mechanism is useful to the purpose of satisfactory diagnosis in MYCIN. It transpires that the mechanism is indeed useful to that purpose; we can ask similar pragmatic questions of other aspects of MYCIN's CF mechanism, and Bayesian mechanisms in general.

One such question is, what are CFs and other numerical degrees of belief used for? These numbers might be used for classification; for example, we might distinguish between "weak," "medium," or "strong" degrees of belief. Second, the numbers might be used for comparison; we might say that one hypothesis is more likely than another. This requires that we have enough confidence in the numbers to accept that i>j is meaningful, even for very small differences between i and j. Note that i>j can be meaningful even if the interpretation of i and j is not known. A third possibility is that i and j might be used as meaningful quantities in their own right; for example, we might interpret j = .7 as the probability of an outcome. Clearly, the interpretation of degrees of belief that involves no assumptions, and that is most tolerant of inaccuracy, is that they are a basis for classification. It seems likely that MYCIN´s insensitivity to inaccurate degrees of belief is due to the fact that it is a classification system. Shortliffe cautions that the CF mechanism is successful for this purpose, but that it should not be blindly adopted for purposes where CFs have a more constrained interpretation.[6] In general, the lesson is that one must ensure that one´s degrees of belief warrant the interpretation they are given: If degrees of belief are interpreted as probabilities, then they must satisfy the requirements of probabilities or lead to errorful results.

Another pragmatic question about numerical degrees of belief is the issue of *representational adequacy*. Does a number represent everything one needs to know about an uncertain situation? An immediate comment is that the range of representations of uncertain situations is somewhat limited. For example, Szolovits and Pauker (1978) note of several medical diagnosis programs:

> The programs rely on a global likelihood assessment scheme, but they use too weak semantics for the states over which they try to compute approximate probabilities. For example, none of the programs can dynamically distinguish among the aggregate hypotheses
>
> 1. A and B, both together, when in fact A has caused B
>
> 2. A and B co-occurring but apparently unrelated, and
>
> 3. A or B but not both.
>
> Yet there are therapeutic and strategic decisions which hinge on just such distinctions. (Szolovits and Pauker, 1978, p. 140)

If, in fact, these three situations should be treated differently by diagnosis systems,

---

[6] My thanks to Professor Shortliffe for proposing these three interpretations of CFs and discussing them with me.

then systems that can do no more than ascribe degrees of belief to A and B suffer from a representational inadequacy.

Although the success of programs like MYCIN suggests strongly that CFs or degrees of belief tell one *enough* about one´s uncertainty to perform well, is it possible that some of the deficits in the performance of these programs can be traced to their representation of uncertainty? I think the answer is yes, and I will give some examples to support this conjecture. The first thing to note about numerical degrees of belief is that they are opaque to a computer program. Whatever reasons an expert has for supplying a degree of belief of .7 are lost to the program that uses the number. Thus, all the questions that one might ask of an expert about his number are lost on the program, and this may well account for the style of explanation that one finds in expert systems. Explanation is handled by reading from a history of inferences. When one asks why a datum or inference is needed, one is told the conclusion that the datum or inference supports (e.g., Shortliffe, 1974, Ch. 6). Explanation systems can tell us how a conclusion was achieved, and how much it is believed. I know of none that can explain its *reasons* for a degree of belief.

A related problem is that numerical degrees of belief probably refer to a wide range of reasons for believing and disbelieving a conclusion, and, worse yet, may not pertain exclusively to belief or certainty at all! A case in point is the confounding of probability and utility in inference rules:

> Most CFs represent a mixture of probabilistic and cost/benefit reasoning. One criticism of MYCIN´s rules has been that utility considerations (in the decision analytic sense) are never made explicit but are "buried" in a rule´s CF. (Buchanan and Shortliffe, 1984, Ch. 10)

This problem is not exclusive to MYCIN, but plagues all approaches to assessment (see Coombs, Dawes, and Tversky, 1970, Ch. 5). Due to MYCIN´s backward-chaining control structure and its predeliction for rules with high CFs, "boosting" a CF had the desired effect of making the system pay attention to it. But this is a convoluted way to control a system and probably should not be considered part of the mechanism for reasoning under uncertainty. The confounding of utility and probability in CFs and presumably in other rules certainly makes explanation difficult. The explanation must necessarily fail to distinguish between pursuing a hypothesis because it is important and because it is likely.

I think it is quite likely that CFs or measures of belief do not have a single interpretation (e.g., "the frequency of x given y is .7"), but rather, are composites of arguments for believing and disbelieving. I may start with a subjective probability of .5, then add something to it due to a couple of very salient cases that happened just yesterday, then subtract something due to self-knowledge that I exagerrate, then add some more because of some perceived utility, and so on. Once we leave the domain of objective probabilities, we must acknowledge that much reasoning and numerous heuristics are involved in assessing a subjective probability.[7] Shafer and Tversky regard assessment of probabilities as constructive:

> We do not think that people come to the task of probability judgment with well-structured beliefs hidden in their psyche and waiting to be "elicited." No doubt they come with some beliefs already formulated. But the process of judgment, when successful, gives new and greater structure to one's beliefs and also tends to render less structured initial beliefs obsolete. So it seems more illuminating to talk about constructing probabilities than to talk about eliciting them. (Shafer and Tversky, 1983, p. 8)

A pragmatic consequence of this view is that if, in fact, degrees of belief are constructed, then intelligent knowledge acquisition systems should help experts with the construction process. This has three positive outcomes. First, knowledge

[7] This point is made cogently and often by numerous authors of articles in Kahneman, Slovic, and Tversky's excellent *Judgment under uncertainty: Heuristics and biases*. 1982.

acquisition may well go faster if an expert is helped to formulate his or her reasons for believing and disbelieving inference rules. Reasons for mistrusting rules might be used to suggest new rules; for example, a useful but too-general rule might be augmented by another with additional conditional clauses. Ideally a knowledge acquisition system such as TEIRESIAS (Davis, 1976) would know that rules can be too general, would offer this to a consulting expert as one of several possible qualifications of a rule, and would then explore with the expert the possibility of another rule that is not too general (see Chapter 5 for further discussion of this approach.) Second, this approach makes reasons for believing and disbelieving rules explicit, so they can be used for explanations and other tasks. Third, the reasons for believing and disbelieving rules, by being explicit, can be useful when several experts contribute to or revise a knowledge base, or when a single expert returns to a rule and asks "Now, why did I think that the degree of belief ought to be .7?"

I have suggested that two difficult and current research problems for expert systems -- explanation and knowledge acquisition -- might be facilitated if degrees of belief are viewed as *constructed*, as the result of cognition, and if the reasons for believing and disbelieving that are usually summarized in degrees of belief are made explicit. Again, I stress that these are pragmatic issues. The final argument for the necessity of a new representation is always pragmatic: We need a new representation to distinguish between situations that were indistinguishable before -- to distinguish utility from probability, to distinguish the effects of salience from corrections for those effects, to distinguish skepticism about an inference rule from the quality of data used in the rule, to distinguish reasons for believing from reasons for disbelieving, and so on. As Szolovits and Pauker noted, above, "There are therapeutic and strategic decisions that rest on just such distinctions." Whenever such a claim is made, another representation of another *kind* of uncertainty is mandated.

These arguments carry over to the next sections, in which we consider the

Dempster-Shafer theory of evidence and fuzzy set theory.

2.2.5 Belief Functions: The Dempster-Shafer Theory of Evidence

The Dempster-Shafer theory, like Bayesian theory, relies on degrees of belief to represent uncertainty. Unlike Bayesian theory, however, it permits one to assign degrees of belief to subsets of hypotheses. In Bayesian theory, one constructs a probability distribution over all individual *singleton* hypotheses, but in the Dempster-Shafer theory, a distribution is constructed over all *subsets* of hypotheses. This is a great advantage. For example, imagine a world with only four automobile makers: Nissan, Toyota, GM, and Chrysler. Imagine also a small, newly developing country, and the hypotheses about who will dominate its automobile sales. In addition to the four singleton hypotheses there are three others: that Japanese auto makers will dominate, that American auto makers will dominate, and that one of the four will dominate. The Dempster-Shafer theory provides us with a language for assigning probabilities to all the hypotheses in this scenario; some of the intuitive assignments permitted by the Dempster-Shafer theory are not handled cleanly in Bayesian theory.

The following example is practically identical to an uncommonly lucid presentation of the Dempster-Shafer theory, written by Gordon and Shortliffe (in Buchanan and Shortliffe, 1984, Ch. 13).

Suppose we obtain evidence that the probability of Japanese dominance is .4. In the Dempster-Shafer theory we can assign the probability .4 to the set {Nissan, Toyota} without committing any of that .4 to either member of the set. In the Bayesian approach we would have to artificially divide the .4 among Nissan and Toyota, with the consequence that we *appear* to know more about their strength in the market than we do know. Furthermore, in the Bayesian scheme, we would be forced to assign the remaining 1 - .4 = .6 of the probability distribution to

American auto makers where it, too, would be divided up among the singleton hypotheses GM and Chrysler. In contrast, the Dempster-Shafer approach allows us to assign the remaining .6 to the set {Nissan Toyota GM Chrysler}, that is, to the set that reflects our ignorance about who will dominate.

The property of the Dempster-Shafer scheme illustrated by this example is that it distinguishes between uncertainty and ignorance. Evidence that Japanese auto makers will dominate a market is just that -- it is *not* evidence about Nissan or Toyota individually, and it certainly isn´t evidence that American auto makers will *not* dominate. Any claim about American auto makers is made out of ignorance, for we have only one piece of evidence, and that is about Japanese auto makers. Ideally, we want to limit our claims to the set {Nissan Toyota}, for which we have evidence of dominance, and to the set {Nissan Toyota GM Chrysler}, that is, the set reflecting our ignorance. The Dempster-Shafer theory permits this assignment because it permits probability distributions over subsets of {Nissan Toyota GM Chrysler}, but the Bayesian theory does not because its probability distribution is constructed over the individual hypotheses {Nissan}, {Toyota}, {GM}, and {Chrysler}.

The largest set from which we construct subsets, the set of all the singletons we know, the set that reflects our ignorance about which singleton is true, is called the *frame of discernment*, and is denoted by Θ. The singletons in Θ are assumed to be mutually exclusive and exhaustive. Θ = {Nissan Toyota GM Chrysler} is the frame of discernment for the problem above. If we have *no* evidence about which subset of Θ will dominate a market, then the probability assigned to Θ is 1.0. To the extent that evidence favors hypotheses constructed from subsets of Θ, such as {Nissan Toyota}, to that extent will the probability assigned to Θ be diminished. The Dempster-Shafer theory introduces a function, called a *basic probability assignment* -- denoted m -- to assign probability to the subsets of Θ. Thus, if our only evidence favors Japanese domination of a market to degree .4, then m({Nissan Toyota}) = .4 and $m(\Theta)$ = .6.

It is desirable to be able to "sum up" the probability assigned to subsets to determine the degree of belief in a superset. For example, imagine we obtain evidence about dominance of a market by GM and Chrysler such that *m*({GM}) = .45 and *m*({Chrysler}) = .15. Then the degree of belief we have in American dominance of a market is:

$$Bel(\{\text{GM Chrysler}\}) = m(\{\text{GM}\}) + m(\{\text{Chrysler}\}) = .45 + .15 = .6$$

Obviously, $Bel(\Theta) = 1.0$, since it is the sum of the basic probability assignments of all subsets of Θ.

To use the Dempster-Shafer theory in a parallel certainty inference architecture, we need a method to incrementally update the values of belief functions Bel_i as evidence becomes available and directs the assignment of probability to subsets of Θ. The mechanism for this is called *Dempster's rule of combination*. Given two pieces of evidence and their probability assignments m_1 and m_2, Dempster's rule provides a way to compute a new probability assignment $m_1 \oplus m_2$ and a new belief function $Bel_1 \oplus Bel_2$. The method is fairly straightforward. Imagine that we have two pieces of evidence about dominance of a market by members of Θ = {Nissan Toyota GM Chrysler}. The first evidence is summarized by *m*({Nissan Toyota}) = .4, and the second by *m*({Toyota GM Chrysler}) = .8. (The latter hypothesis illustrates the method used by Dempster and Shafer to represent *negations*: *m*({Toyota GM Chrysler}) = m_i makes assignments not only to its subset of Θ, but also to Θ itself. That is, prior to combination, m_1 assigns .4 to {Nissan Toyota} and .6 to Θ; and m_2 assigns .8 to {Toyota GM Chrysler} and .2 to Θ. Intuitively, it seems that since we have two pieces of evidence about Toyota, we should be able to make a probability assignment to {Toyota} alone; in fact, it seems that we should assign a pretty good probability to Toyota, since the assignment made by m_2 does not favor Nissan. Then, too, if we are able to make a probability assignment to Toyota, we should *reduce* the probability assigned to {Toyota GM Chrysler}, because a good chunk of the .8 assigned by m_2, we now realize, was assigned on behalf of Toyota. Similarly, we should reduce the probability assignment to {Nissan Toyota}. Table 2-1 shows an arrangement that embodies these intuitive arguments.

		m_2	
		{Toyota GM Chrysler}(0.8)	Θ(0.2)
m_1	{Nissan Toyota}(0.4)	{Toyota}(0.32)	{Nissan Toyota}(0.8)
	Θ(0.6)	{Toyota GM Chrysler}(0.48)	Θ(0.12)

Table 2.1: Tableau for Dempster's Rule of Combination

In each cell of the table we put the intersection of two sets: The intersection of {Toyota GM Chrysler} and {Nissan Toyota} is {Toyota}; the intersection of Θ and Θ is Θ; the intersection of Θ and any subset of Θ is that subset. We then simply multiply the probability assignments of the original sets to achieve the probability assignment for their intersection. Thus, $m_1 \oplus m_2$({Toyota}) = 0.32, $m_1 \oplus m_2$({Nissan Toyota}) = 0.08, $m_1 \oplus m_2$({Toyota GM Chrysler}) = 0.48, and $m_1 \oplus m_2(\Theta)$ = 0.12. Belief functions are calculated as before. Thus, belief that the Japanese will dominate a market is

$$Bel_1 \oplus Bel_2(\{\text{Nissan Toyota})\} =$$
$$m_1 \oplus m_2(\{\text{Nissan Toyota}\}) + m_1 \oplus m_2(\{\text{Nissan}\}) + m_1 \oplus m_2(\{\text{Toyota}\}) =$$
$$0.8 + 0.0 + 0.32 = 0.4$$

This simple scheme gives rise to a number of complications that will not be discussed here. For further discussion of the theory, see Gordon and Shortliffe (in Buchanan and Shortliffe, 1984, Ch. 13); Barnett (1981); and Shafer (1976).

2.2.6 Fuzzy Logic as an Approach to Vagueness

Many of the words and phrases in our written and spoken language are vague. We speak of "cold" beer, "high" interest rates, and "intelligent" colleagues, but we do not wish to specify the temperature at which beer ceases to be cold, the percentage at which interest ceases to be high, or the behavior that qualifies a colleague as intelligent. It is only when we force these terms to express binary distinctions that their vagueness becomes problematic. We all know how a cold beer looks and tastes, but is there any sensory test that is capable of telling us exactly when a glass of beer passes the point of being cold and becomes warm? If 38 F. is cold, is 39 F. *not* cold? When I leave a cold glass of beer to sit in the sunshine, the beer gets warm gradually. There is no fixed point at which my beer ceases to be a member of the class of "cold" objects.

But if we accept that there are terms for which there is not an exact definition, sets for which there are not precise membership criteria, then we introduce uncertainty. In previous sections we have seen how uncertainty can be represented as a probability, which sets up a correspondence between the uncertain situation and the idea of random variables -- variables whose values are the outcome of a random process. This is not entirely appropriate for terms like "cold." We do not think of "cold" as, say, an interval of a probability distribution of temperatures. Rather, our uncertainty arises from not knowing precisely the temperature range denoted by "cold." Obviously, we manage very well with this uncertainty because the term "cold" has an agreed-upon if indefinite meaning. But, if we are to use the term and others like it in AI programs, how can we specify their meaning? For any precise definition of a vague term there will always be a handful of cases that come within an iota of satisfying the definition but are rejected -- cases that we would agree satisfy the definition "nearly enough" to be used. What we need is a "fuzzy" definition, such that a glass of beer is "more or less cold" depending on its temperature.

The term "fuzzy" was introduced by Lotfi Zadeh (1965) to describe sets whose membership criteria are imprecise (see also Gaines, 1976, for an overview of developments since.) The idea is that an object is not simply in or out of a set, but has a degree of membership. Thus, warmish beer is only marginally a member of the set of cold things. Uncertainty about a statement, such as "the beer is cold," is not represented by the *probability* that the beer is cold, but rather by what Zadeh (1978) calls the *possibility* that the beer is cold. The possibility of a statement is represented by a number generated by a *membership function.* For example, we can imagine values of the membership function μ for temperatures of beer: The degree of membership of 38 F. beer in the class of cold beer is 1 ($\mu[38] = 1$), but for 46 F. beer is only .2 ($\mu[46] = .2$)

Zadeh has axiomatized possibility theory so that it has analogs for most constructs in probability theory. In principle, the two can be used in much the same way. There is a FUZZY programming language (LeFaivre, 1977), and apparently a couple of AI applications were developed in it (Barr and Feigenbaum, 1982). But relatively little has been made of the idea of fuzzy sets and possibility theory in AI. Buchanan and Duda (1982) suggest this may be because the idea does not improve upon any of the difficult methodological problems that beset probability theory (see section 2.2.4), such as assessment of prior probabilities.

2.2.7 Control Approaches to Uncertainty

It is not necessary to represent one's state of certainty to solve problems under uncertainty: Much uncertainty succumbs to solving a problem by following an appropriately designed *control strategy.* Control strategies specify what a problem solver should do next. By exploiting properties of an uncertain domain in the design of a control strategy, one can reduce the effects of uncertainty. As an illustration, consider the possible control strategies for solving a jigsaw puzzle: One can work on "anything" next, or one can attempt to build the frame of the puzzle first -- exploiting the fact that frame pieces have at least one straight edge. Having built the frame one can again work on "anything" next, or one can search for puzzle pieces that extend the frame inwards -- exploiting the property that puzzle pieces fit together. Usually, the strategy of building the frame first and working inwards will solve the puzzle faster than the "do anything first" strategy. In both cases, there is uncertainty about the placement of any given puzzle piece, but with a smart control strategy we can "grade" this uncertainty: Edge pieces are least uncertain and should be worked in first, and then any piece that looks as if it might extend the frame is less uncertain than another piece whose placement is completely unconstrained.

The control approach to uncertainty is often used when the goal is to interpret noisy, but converging, evidence. For example, line-finding algorithms for image understanding must contend with noisy image data, but sometimes use the partially-understood image as a source of expectations to guide further processing of the image (e.g., Shirai, 1973; Kanade and Shafer, 1982). Similarly, expectations and data converge on interpretations of speech in HEARSAY-II and other speech understanding systems (see Erman, Hayes-Roth, Lesser, and Reddy, 1980; Lea, 1980; Barr and Feigenbaum, 1981). In these systems, the decision to attend to a hypothesis or ignore it is related to how certain the hypothesis is: The systems are said to establish and extend *islands of certainty*; those parts, or islands, of a spoken utterance that are relatively certain are used to guide understanding of the rest of the utterance.

Uncertainty influences the behavior of the system in a control approach to uncertainty. The influence of uncertainty on the behavior of systems that use the degree-of-belief approach (see section 2.2.3) is minimal. For example, MYCIN did not pursue any hypothesis with a CF of less than 0.2, and thus made a rudimentary discrimination on which it based a simple control decision (Shortliffe, 1974). But, in general, uncertainty has a passive existence in systems of the MYCIN ilk, and a much more active role in the control approach to uncertainty.

I have argued elsewhere that one cannot expect a system to use uncertainty to control its processing when the only information available about the uncertainty is a degree of belief (Cohen and Grinberg, 1983); so we would expect that systems like HEARSAY-II and Shirai's line-finder must reason with information in addition to degrees of belief in hypotheses. The most important information for these systems may be the set of partially developed hypotheses. This information -- the set of partial interpretations of some speech or visual information -- is what these systems build upon as they work. Provided there is redundancy in the evidence available to the systems, the effects of incorrect partial interpretations can be minimized. The corpus of partial interpretations is so important to further control decisions that HEARSAY-II -- which initially was designed for very flexible and autonomous control -- had to follow a prescribed control regimen to build up an initial set of hypotheses.

The following section discusses a general, and now quite common, architecture for AI systems. This is the *blackboard* control structure, developed during the HEARSAY project (Erman and Lesser, 1975), and since applied to numerous problems of interpreting noisy data. For example, Engelmore and Terry, (1979) describe the blackboard architecture in X-ray crystallography; Nii and Feigenbaum (1978) present a blackboard approach to signal understanding; Hanson and Riseman (1978) discuss a comprehensive model of vision; Rumelhart (1976) describes a psychological model of reading; Hayes-Roth and Hayes-Roth (1979) apply the blackboard model to planning; and, Nii and Aiello (1979) describe the AGE system for developing blackboard models.

2.2.8 The Blackboard Model

Classic blackboard models have a modular architecture consisting of several *knowledge sources*, a *database* or blackboard, and a *scheduler*. The knowledge sources (KSs) are collections of production rules, grouped by their *stimulus* and *response frames*. For example, all the rules in a knowledge source, say KS1, may test some characteristic of the phonetic structure of an utterance, and specify some characteristic of the syllable structure of the utterance. Then, the stimulus frame of KS1 is all those hypotheses on the blackboard that pertain to phonetic structure. Blackboards are typically organized into levels that correspond to the stimulus and response frames of KSs; so, the *syllable* level is the response frame for KS1.

Knowledge sources can be thought to scan the blackboard for newly posted hypotheses that match their stimulus frames. When this happens, one or more rules in a KS may have their conditions matched and, thus, be prepared to contribute a hypothesis (the rule´s conclusion) to the blackboard. This sounds like a straightforward, data-directed, forward-chaining control structure, and indeed it would be but for the scheduler:

> One objective of *attentional control* is to schedule the numerous potential activities of the KSs to prevent the intractable combinatorial explosion that would inevitably result from an unconstrained application of KSs. (Hayes-Roth and Lesser, 1977)

Unfortunately, the scheduling of KSs in blackboard models, though the most important factor in control, can be ad hoc. In HEARSAY-II, for example, a system was developed that scored each KS on the extent to which it satisfied five control principles, such as *the best of several local alternatives should be performed first*. In contrast, the HWIM (Hear What I Mean) system (Wolf and Woods, 1980) -- which is not strictly a blackboard model -- was designed to support explicit control strategies, in contrast to the abstract and implicit strategy embodied in HEARSAY-II´s control principles.

Whether implicit or explicit, control strategies can be designed to minimize uncertainty in noisy domains. The blackboard architecture facilitates control structure design in two ways. First, knowledge is kept in modular knowledge sources which communicate only through the blackboard. Thus, the flow of information (and the potential of combinatorial proliferation of same) is easy to control. Second, the blackboard contains a great deal of information, both as explicit hypotheses and implicit in its structure; for example, many blackboard models have *time* as a dimension, so it is easy to see whether hypotheses refer to the same part of an utterance or a signal. Given this information and control over the addition of information to the blackboard from knowledge sources, one can design control structures that focus a system's efforts on tasks that will reduce its uncertainty. For example, the designers of HWIM discovered that sentences have a semantic structure such that they are more easily understood by starting two or three words into the sentence, then working back to the beginning, then continuing from the middle (the *middle-out* strategy). The HEARSAY-II designers adopted a similar *island-driving* strategy, where fairly certain fragments of the utterance were identified and then speculative links between them were proposed. These strategies are not unlike the strategy for solving jigsaw puzzles above, and the principle is the same.

More recently, there have been proposals that blackboard-based systems should reason about their own control (Corkill, 1983), that is, KSs should be included whose expertise is in focussing the attention of the system. This proposal comes very close to the principle in SOLOMON that endorsements should be used for control decisions (see Section 4.5).

Control of processing in the abstract blackboard architecture is *asynchronous* and thus can be *opportunistic*. What this means is that KSs are not activated in any particular order, but rather, they contribute hypotheses in response to situations on the blackboard. Consequently, the KSs can take advantage of opportunities to contribute to a problem as they arise. This asynchrony and opportunism is what facilitates the *island-driving* style of processing. It is an especially powerful approach for uncertain situations because, if KSs are constrained to work on parts of a problem in a fixed order, regardless of whether they have anything to contribute, they will post conclusions that will have to be undone later. This backtracking problem can be minimized by allowing KSs to contribute when they are ready.

Blackboard models are not the only control approaches to uncertainty. The principle of designing a control strategy to exploit some property of a problem domain -- such as straight edges on jigsaw puzzle pieces or the fact that edges of polyhedra are straight -- is found in many problem solvers. What follows are three examples from the AI literature.

Least Commitment Planning. A very basic kind of uncertainty is the control question of what to do next. In planning problems it often happens that one planned action interferes with another (e.g., Sussman, 1975). However, the space of all possible sequences of actions is usually too large to search for one that does not exhibit interference between actions. There is thus real uncertainty about the order in which actions should be tried. One can either adopt a "do anything next" control strategy that may lead to interactions, which may themselves be reparable; or, one can adopt the least commitment strategy of *not* adopting an ordering of actions until there are stated reasons to do one action before another. The latter control structure facilitates planning because it avoids costly backtracking. It exploits the characteristic that actions constrain each other (if only by interfering with each other.) Sacerdoti (1977) and Stefik (1981) developed planning systems that used the least commitment approach.

The Method of Assumed States and Dependency-Directed Backtracking. Stallman and Sussman (1976) describe a program, EL, that must *guess* the states of electrical components in circuits. This is called the method of assumed states, and is apparently a technique used by expert electrical engineers. A consequence of guessing wrongly is that the hypothetical circuit will exhibit inconsistent states; for example, a wire may have a high voltage at one end and low one at the other. In such a case, there is uncertainty about which of several assumptions is responsible for the inconsistency and about which new assumption would avoid inconsistencies.

Stallman and Sussman developed a control structure, called dependency-directed backtracking, that coped with these uncertainties much more efficiently than PLANNER-type, chronological backtracking (Hewitt, 1971). When a contradiction is discovered, EL decides to withdraw the assumption that it thinks is most *likely* to be wrong. Interestingly, this kind of backtracking behavior -- returning to the point most likely to be wrong -- has been found by Carpenter and Just (1981) for recovery from reading errors in human subjects.

Agendas. A mechanism similar to the blackboard is called an *agenda*, and was developed by Lenat (1976) for control of his AM system. AM is a program that characterizes discovery in mathematics as a search in a space of concepts. It develops *huge* numbers of concepts, and needs to control which ones it looks at. Concepts have associated *reasons* to be examined, and these reasons have numerical weights. AM uses a simple formula to rate concepts on the agenda, so it can avoid looking at those concepts that don't rate. A crude characterization of AM's problem is to say that it is always uncertain about what concepts to work on next, and that its uncertainty is represented not by a probability but by heuristically-derived ratings (i.e., by an ad hoc scoring scheme). This scheme has some characteristics in common with the model of endorsement, and is discussed in more detail in the next section.

2.3 The Model of Endorsement

The explicit marking of factors relating to one's certainty is called *endorsement*. The records of these factors are called endorsements. This section provides an overview of the model of endorsement. It does not go into the details of knowledge representation or mechanisms for reasoning with endorsements (these are discussed in Chapter 4); rather, it presents the general ideas of the model in terms of two analogies, outlines the design of a program that implements the model, discusses some of the research issues, and reviews some pertinent literature.

2.3.1 Two Analogies for the Model of Endorsement

Shafer and Tversky (1983) point out that the semantics of a probability theory provides one with, among other things, "mental devices" to facilitate comparisons of the situation at hand with the scale of probabilities. For example, if we adopt a frequency semantics for probability, we may employ the mental device of a spinning pointer that comes to rest in some randomly determined sector of a disk. We may use this device to help us interpret the statement P(A) = .9. The interpretation is facilitated by the mental image that the disk is painted red in one sector and blue in the other, and that red sector is nine times bigger the blue. Then, the interpretation of P(A) = .9 is "my support for A is comparable to what would be provided by associating A with the red sector and spinning the pointer."[8] The mental device of a spinner on a disk not only helps one interpret P(A) = .9 with the frequency semantics, but also helps us think about whether the frequency semantics is *appropriate* for the situation we are trying to represent.

One mental device or analogy by which to introduce the model of endorsement is that of a bureaucracy. A piece of work in a bureaucracy proceeds from one stage to the next contingent on the endorsement of a bureaucrat. The job must satisfy certain (typically formal) requirements before it is endorsed at any given level. Imagine, in place of bureaucrats watching over a job, a collection of rules watching over the development of a line of reasoning. Each endorses a step in the argument if it satisfies certain requirements. Whenever a domain rule is used, its conclusion accrues one or more endorsements. Thus, *endorsements* are just records that a particular kind of inference has taken place, and *endorsers* are just

[8] There are other semantics for probability statements; Shortliffe and Buchanan (1975), for example, discuss several.

the computations that assert the records. Bureaucrats can require a job to be cleared by lesser bureaucrats before they even consider it; for example, a city council won´t consider a proposal unless it is cleared by the planning department, and they won´t look at it unless the lawyers have approved it first. Similarly, an endorser may require the conditions of a rule to have a certain level of endorsement before it will endorse the conclusion of the rule. For example, one endorser might endorse the conclusions of a rule only if the conditions were themselves endorsed as parameters derived from rules that do not introduce uncertainty, such as simple arithmetic transformations. Most conclusions accrue several, more or less stringent endorsements. The certainty of a hypothesis can be represented as its strongest endorsement. In terms of the bureaucracy analogy, one´s confidence in a job is proportional to the degree of scrutiny and level through which it has passed.

Accrual of endorsements as if by independent bureaucrats is a useful way to view the evidence pro and con a hypothesis, but how shall we extend the analogy to the process of *weighing* evidence? We can imagine the bureaucrats arranging themselves on opposite ends of a seesaw, or in a tug-of-war. "Weighty" or "strong" endorsements will count disproportionately in the contest, as is desirable. A more passive but essentially equivalent analogy is that of a ledger book. The book has three columns, one for evidence in favor of a hypothesis, one for evidence against the hypothesis, and one for irrelevant evidence. Weighing evidence then has two stages: First, decide in which column a piece of evidence belongs, and, second, do the "accounting" of the evidence pro and con. Endorsements, we shall see, are structures associated with evidence that provide one with the information necessary for these operations.

2.3.2 Design Criteria for the Model of Endorsement

In this section, the model of endorsement and the SOLOMON program are discussed as if they were the same thing. In fact, there is much to the model of endorsement that remains unimplemented in SOLOMON. Wherever such a discrepancy arises, it is noted.

The primary design goal for the model of endorsement is that knowledge *about* uncertain situations should influence the behavior of the system. An important behavior is deciding what to do when one lacks the evidence one needs. In the model of endorsement, this involves designing *resolution tasks*. A resolution task is one whose execution either *reduces* uncertainty, usually by obtaining more information, or *discounts* or somehow lessens the impact of the uncertainty. For example, King Solomon lacked evidence about the true mother of the baby. However, he was able to exploit other knowledge about his uncertainty -- particularly recognition of the *kind* of uncertainty -- to help him design the experiment that ultimately led to a resolution of his uncertainty.

Consonant with this primary design goal is the criterion that uncertainty should affect control decisions. The control problem is basically "what shall I work on next?" SOLOMON tries not to work on tasks that will not increase its certainty in one or more conclusions. Thus, before it starts to work on a task it asks whether the task contributes anything; furthermore, when it schedules tasks on its agenda it does so by asking what it expects them to contribute to its certainty. As with other control approaches to uncertainty (see section 2.2.7), these behaviors may not solve uncertain problems, but they do exploit knowledge *about* the uncertainty to facilitate resolutions. In the first case -- where tasks are screened before being executed -- SOLOMON uses knowledge of the interrelationships of tasks and of conclusions. For example, if a task concludes something that is already believable, then there is no point executing it. The second case -- where tasks are scheduled on the agenda by asking which is most likely to contribute to the system´s certainty -- requires a priori knowledge derived from inference rules. When an expert provides a rule for SOLOMON, he also gives some reasons why the rule can be used with more or less confidence, and these reasons are used to schedule execution of the rule (see section 4.5).

An engineering goal is that, if possible, SOLOMON´s skill with uncertainty should result primarily from its knowledge about uncertainty, and that its control structure should involve minimal modification of structures already common in AI programs. I was eager to avoid the "control approach" to uncertainty, discussed in section 2.2.7, because it keeps knowledge about uncertainty implicit. I also thought that the promise of endorsement-based approach would be more obvious if it was framed in a common control structure. For these reasons, I chose backward-chaining as SOLOMON´s control structure (see section 2.3.3.2 for an introduction to backward-chaining). Forward-chaining was another possibility, especially since SOLOMON´s original application, FOLIO, is a forward-chaining system. Backward-chaining has the advantage that that it involves recursive generation of subgoals, and thus provides a natural mechanism for asking "what goal is this uncertain result intended to satisfy; what do I want to use the result for?"

Another design goal for the model of endorsement is that one´s certainty in a result should depend on what the result is wanted for. Imagine that King Solomon is to judge a case of alleged murder. We might expect that his courtiers, betting among themselves that he will judge guilty or not-guilty, might be more sanguine than Solomom himself, since as observers -- whose personal judgment may cost them a bet but not the defendent´s life -- they need less evidence to be convinced of guilt. SOLOMON accepts evidence in one context and rejects it as wanting in another. For example, it accepts relatively poor evidence for clauses that are not necessary to inferences (so-called *supportive* clauses; see section 4.4.1.1), but rejects the use of the same evidence for other kinds of clauses.

Since a proposition might be thought to have adequate evidence in one context but not another, the common interpretations of "true" and "false" have been modified. Data and conclusions in SOLOMON are either "certain enough for the task at hand," or they are not. Moreover, since the adequacy of evidence changes with context, a design decision for SOLOMON is that *all* conclusions should be asserted in the database, regardless of whether they are *currently* believable. When SOLOMON attempts to use a conclusion, it evaluates its believability in the current context, rather than relying on a previous evaluation. This is because believable conclusions may become less believable, and initially unbelievable conclusions may become "certain enough." The believability of propositions changes with two general events: A conclusion may not be certain enough for one purpose but may be adequate for another, so that changing one's goals affects the usefulness of conclusions. Secondly, conclusions that affect the believability of current conclusions may be added to the database; for example, a conclusion becomes more believable if corroborating evidence is added to the database, and less believable if a contradicting conclusion is added.

Currently, SOLOMON does not use any numbers to reason about uncertainty. The model of endorsement does not preclude endorsements that include numerical measures such as degrees of belief. But my goal has been to see how far one can go with qualitative reasons for believing and disbelieving – with symbolic endorsements – to the exclusion of representations of intensity or strength or degree of belief. By doing this we engage in an experiment: The goal is to see whether degrees of belief are necessary to reasoning about uncertainty. Current systems lack any knowledge about uncertainty *but* degrees of belief; is it possible that these can be entirely replaced by the reasons that they summarize?

SOLOMON was designed to use very general knowledge as well as domain-specific methods for reasoning about uncertainty. To this end, SOLOMON's knowledge is organized hierarchically, with general methods acting as defaults when more specific methods are lacking. Initially, SOLOMON was intended to engage in sophisticated reasoning about the uncertainty implicit in portfolio management, but this domain did not afford the characteristics needed to test the model of endorsement. Thus, the goal of the SOLOMON effort became to develop a general corpus of knowledge about uncertainty that could be used for building expert systems in a variety of uncertain domains. Since this knowledge is structured and explicit, we will eventually be able to develop a meta-language to describe endorsements. This should allow acquisition of knowledge about uncertainty from domain experts in much the way that TEIRESIAS (Davis, 1976) acquired domain rules.

These design goals can be summarized very briefly: One should represent what one knows about uncertain situations, and use the knowledge to find methods for resolving the uncertainty. Knowledge about uncertainty should play an *active* role in controlling reasoning about and resolution of uncertainty. One's belief in a proposition should depend in part on what the proposition is wanted for: A proposition may be believable enough to function as a premise in an inconsequential inference, but it may be rejected for more serious purposes. Thus, propositions are not "true" or "false" but are more or less believable, depending on the evidence they accrue and the purposes for which they are used. Knowledge about uncertainty should be explicit and carefully structured; and, as an experiment, it should rely minimally on numerical degrees of belief.

2.3.3 Architecture of SOLOMON

The model of endorsement specifies the knowledge and control structures necessary for a computational model of reasoning about uncertainty. The model is intended to provide an *architecture* in which to build AI programs. By architecture we mean a representation for knowledge about uncertainty and a control structure that specifies how the knowledge is to be used to solve problems. These will be discussed in the following sections; first, we present short descriptions of predicate calculus notation and backward chaining, since these tools will be used throughout the document. Readers familiar with these topics are encouraged to skip to the next section.

2.3.3.1 Predicate Calculus Notation

The predicate calculus provides a simple representation for propositions that can be assigned truth values. Such propositions include "Degas was an impressionist," and "Two heads are better than one," but not "Degas´ daughter" or "Two heads," because the latter propositions are not true or false. Propositions in predicate calculus are true when the *predicate* of a proposition is true of its *arguments*. The predicate is usually the first term in a proposition and the arguments follow. Thus, **(impressionist degas)** says that the predicate **impressionist** is true of the object **degas,** and **(better-than two-heads one-head)** says that the predicate **better-than** is true of the list **(two-heads one-head)**. Note that predicates can have more than one argument, and that when they do, the order of the arguments is significant.

One often wishes to reason about variables, as well as constants such as **degas**. This is easily accomplished: We might write **((artist x)** => **(impressionist x))**, to denote that if **x** is an an artist, then **x** is an impressionist. There is some ambiguity, however, about whether we mean *all* artists are impressionists, or whether just *some* artists are impressionists. If we mean the former we write **Forall x (artist x)** => **(impressionist x)**, which means that any **x** that satisfies the predicate **artist x** also satisfies **impressionist x.** If we mean the latter we write **Exists x (artist x)** => **(impressionist x)**, which is true if there exists at least one **x** that is an impressionist (or if not, there should be no **x**s that are artists.) The first form is called *universal quantification*, and the latter *existential quantification*.

The rules in this document are all of the form **If premise, Then conclusion**, where **premise** and **conclusion** are statements in the predicate calculus. Terms preceded by a question mark are universally quantified variables. For example, the rule **If (income ?client high) Then (tax-bracket ?client high)** says, "For any individual **?client**, if **?client** has a high level of income, then the tax-bracket of **?client** is high."

2.3.3.2 The Backward Chaining Control Structure

Consider four abstract inference rules:

v => **w**, **w** => **y**, **x** => **y** and **y** => **z**.

How can one prove **z**? The premise of **z** is **y**, so if one can prove **y**, then one can prove **z**. Similarly, **y** depends on proving either **w** or **x**, and **w** depends on proving **v**. To prove **z**, then, we might ask first whether there are any inference rules that conclude **z** and, finding the single rule {**y** => **z**} we enquire whether the rule´s premise, **y**, is true. If so, the problem is solved. If not, we pose a new problem, namely, to prove **y**. We proceed with this problem in exactly the same manner as with **z**: We search for all inference rules that conclude **y**, which yields the set {**w** => **y**, **x** => **y**}, and ask whether the preconditions of either of *these* rules is true. If so, the problem is solved. If not, we try to find rules that conclude **w**, or **x**. This yields the single rule {**v** => **w**}, which we test as with the other rules.

Backward chaining is the strategy of trying to prove a rule´s conclusion by finding all inferences that conclude the rule´s premise, and trying to prove each of those inferences in turn. A central procedure in backward chaining is called *unification*; it is responsible for finding the inference rules whose conclusions match a desired premise. For example, *we* can see that the conclusion of **x** => **y** matches the premise of **y** => **z**, but the basis for this match must be explained to a computer. The terms **y** and **x** are too simple to illustrate unification. Imagine, instead, that we are trying to prove that a person, Fred, should have few taxable bonds. First, we search for rules that conclude about having few taxable bonds, and find

(If (tax-bracket ?client high)
Then (taxable-bond-need ?client low)).

Recall (from section 2.3.3.1) that **?client** is a variable. So, if we are trying to prove that *Fred* needs few taxable bonds, we can use this rule with Fred *substituted* for **?client**. Given a proposition, such as **(taxable-bond-need Fred low)**, the process of unification finds other propositions for which there is a valid *substitution* of constants for variables. Thus, the conclusion of the rule above unifies with our goal **(taxable-bond-need Fred low)** under the substitution **((?client / Fred))**. One useful property of the unification procedure is that we can use this substitution to produce the next goal, which, in a backward chaining system, is always the premise of the rule one wishes to use. The premise of the rule above is *instantiated* with the substitution, so that we next attempt to prove the goal **(tax-bracket Fred high)**. Now consider the rule:

(If (income ?person ?level)
Then (tax-bracket ?person ?level)).

Unification finds that this rule´s conclusion matches the goal **(tax-bracket Fred high)** under the substitution **(?person / Fred)(?level / high)**. This substitution is used to produce the next goal, which is the instantiated premise of the rule above: **(income Fred high)**.

Thus, the unification process allows us to write rules with variables, but use them with individuals – such as **Fred** – or other constant terms. This is obviously a great efficiency. Imagine, for example, the number of rules one would require instead of the previous rule, if all relevant **?levels** had to be spelled out. The predicate calculus and unification are presented very clearly in Nilsson´s excellent introductions to AI (1971, 1980).

2.3.3.3 Control in SOLOMON

SOLOMON´s control structure, in broad terms, is illustrated in Figure 2-2.

(See also the main control functions in Fig. 4-1.)

Tasks. SOLOMON works with *tasks* that are designed to satisfy goals. Tasks have a *conclusion* and a *condition*; the former is a goal that is achieved when the latter is established. For example, if SOLOMON wants to determine someone´s tax-bracket, it searches among its domain rules and finds one for inferring tax-bracket, say, **"If income is high, then income tax is high."** From this rule it generates the *subtask* of determining the person´s income. Another kind of task is a *resolution* task. These are responses to uncertainty, and often involve modifying extant tasks in which SOLOMON lacks confidence. For example, the conditions of two tasks may be merged if their conclusions potentially corroborate, or a clause may be dropped from a condition if it is not necessary and SOLOMON is having difficulty satisfying it.

The Database. Inference systems such as SOLOMON maintain a database of propositions or statements that are believed to be true. Initial data are stored in the database, as are conclusions derived as the inference system reasons. SOLOMON differs from most systems in that the propositions in its database cannot be assumed to be true. Each is judged on the basis of its endorsement and, in fact, statements are asserted in the database even if they have very poor support.

The Agenda. SOLOMON puts its tasks on an agenda in an order determined by their endorsements. Tasks are derived from inference rules, and the endorsements of these rules are used to schedule the tasks on SOLOMON´s agenda (step 8, Fig. 2-2). Tasks from strongly endorsed rules are scheduled ahead of those from weakly endorsed rules. This is analogous to scheduling rules with a high numerical degree of belief (or possibly a high degree of disbelief) before less compelling rules. A scheduling algorithm for tasks is discussed in sections 2.3.4 and 4.3.3.1.

Screening. When a task is taken off the agenda to be run, SOLOMON checks whether it is still worth running (step 2, Fig. 2-2). Tasks that appeared worthwhile when they were scheduled may have become redundant in the interim. Currently, SOLOMON will not pursue a task whose conclusion has already been derived by a previous task, and is believable. This is a special case of screening. In general, SOLOMON is intended to eliminate tasks that do not contribute enough to its certainty in one or more conclusions. In these cases, if the best-endorsed task on the agenda is not well-enough endorsed, SOLOMON tries to generate a new resolution task that will be better endorsed (step 6, Fig. 2-2).

Satisfying conditions. (Step 3, Fig. 2-2). In rule-based inference systems like SOLOMON, the conclusion of a rule is asserted if the condition of the rule is satisfied. In general, a condition is satisfied if it matches a statement in the database. SOLOMON permits considerable control over what it means for statements to match. Furthermore, a match does not in itself satisfy a condition, because SOLOMON must first check whether the matching statement in the database is believable. Unlike other systems, SOLOMON asserts the conclusion of a rule even if its condition is *not* satisfied, but it expresses its mistrust in the endorsement of the conclusion.

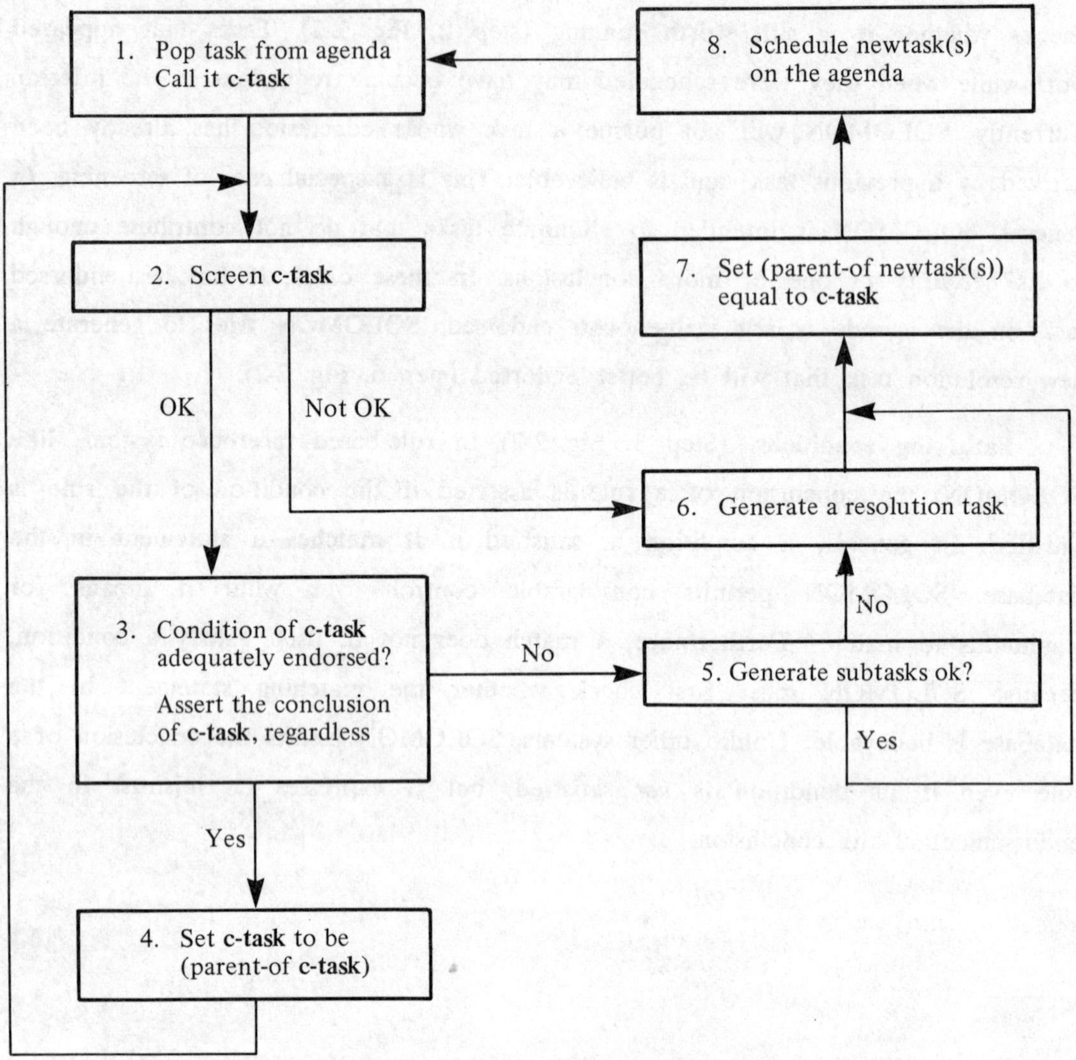

Figure 2.2: Flow of Control in the SOLOMON Program

Back chaining. Tasks are generally proposed to establish the conditions of other tasks. For example, if **x=>y**, and **y=>z**, then to establish **z** we must conclude **y**, which results in the task of inferring **y** from **x**. The initial task, inferring **z** from **y**, is called the *parent* task, and the subsequent task, inferring **y** from **x**, is called the *subtask* or child task. Whenever a subtask is satisfied, we want to back up to the parent to see if it is satisfied, too. (It might not be, because other clauses in its condition may not yet have been established by subtasks.) This back-up is illustrated by the arc in Figure 2-2 between step 4 and step 2. SOLOMON does indeed reschedule the parent task.

Generating subtasks. In the event that a task´s condition is not satisfied, SOLOMON searches its rules for those that will conclude the desired condition (step 5, Fig. 2-2). For example, in the previous paragraph we saw that **z** could not be immediately asserted because **y** was not satisfied. In that case, another rule that concluded **y** was found and a subtask generated. If SOLOMON is unable to generate subtasks in this fashion, it will attempt to generate a resolution task. (If this fails, it will simply return to the agenda and attempt the next task.) Subtasks or resolution tasks are linked to the parent task that required them (step 7, Fig. 2-2), and then are scheduled on the agenda (step 8, Fig. 2-2).

Terminating conditions. SOLOMON stops work when its agenda is empty. After it has successfully established its top-level goal, it successively discards all agenda tasks with the screening procedure (step 2, Fig. 2-2). As long as the top-level goal is not achieved, SOLOMON screens and executes agenda tasks.

2.3.3.4 Knowledge in SOLOMON

The style of processing outlined in the previous section requires several different kinds of knowledge. These are:

Domain Inference Rules from a Base System. SOLOMON is not itself an expert system, but is intended eventually as an "E-system" in the style of EMYCIN (van Melle, 1980). The system builder encodes domain expertise in SOLOMON just as in EMYCIN, but SOLOMON provides more sophisticated reasoning about uncertainty. Currently, the model of endorsement is designed to facilitate reasoning about uncertainty in backward-chaining, rule-based inference systems. The approach of this research has been to re-code parts of FOLIO in SOLOMON. In future, I anticipate building expert systems from scratch in SOLOMON.

Endorsements. These are the data structures that summarize reasons for believing and disbelieving domain inferences. Endorsements also specify information about matching for use by SOLOMON's unification algorithm. (See sections 4.4.1.3 and 4.4.)

Rules for Scheduling Agenda Tasks. Rule-endorsements are used to rank tasks on SOLOMON's agenda. SOLOMON uses simple rules about which rule endorsements are preferred. This is part of the more general problem of ranking endorsements (see sections 2.3.4 and 4.3.3.1).

Rules for Screening Agenda Tasks. When a task is popped from the agenda, SOLOMON checks whether it still contributes anything. Tasks that make redundant conclusions are abandoned. This and other criteria for screening agenda tasks are discussed in section 4.3.3.2.

Rules for Propagating Endorsements over Inferences. If **P** implies **Q** and the endorsements of **P** are the set $\mathbf{e_P}$, then what are the endorsements of **Q**? Currently, the set $\mathbf{e_Q}$ contains the endorsements of the inference **(P=>Q)**, any evidential relationships between **Q** and other conclusions in the database, and the set $\mathbf{e_P}$. This latter component of $\mathbf{e_Q}$ grows combinatorially during a chain of inferences. Thus, the rules for propagating endorsements over inferences must ultimately contain heuristics for *dropping*, *replacing*, or *combining* endorsements.

Rules to Determine Whether a Proposition is Certain Enough. SOLOMON is continually checking whether hypotheses have adequate support (whether they are *well-endorsed*). This is facilitated by rules that are sensitive to context. For example, SOLOMON has a general rule that if **((and $\mathbf{P_1}$ $\mathbf{P_2}$)=>Q)** is an inference rule, and the rule condition endorsements of $\mathbf{P_1}$ and $\mathbf{P_2}$ are **necessary** and **supportive**, respectively, then the endorsement of the proposition that proves $\mathbf{P_1}$ must be stronger than that of the proposition that proves $\mathbf{P_2}$. Said differently, evidence that is adequate in the context of trying to conclude a supportive clause, may be inadequate in the context of trying to conclude a necessary clause.

Rules to Propose Resolution Tasks. When no task on the agenda provides adequate support for a proposition, SOLOMON is able to design new tasks specifically to provide support and break the impasse. This may involve combining old tasks´ condition clauses, dropping condition clauses, changing the necessary level of endorsement, and so on. Currently, SOLOMON has rules to recognize types of impasses; the conclusions of these rules call procedures for building new tasks.

This ends the introduction to SOLOMON. We now consider some of the research issues that arise frequently in this document.

2.3.4 Research Issues for the Model of Endorsement

One may anticipate a number of questions about the model of endorsement: How can endorsements be *weighed* if they are not numbers? What is the *net weight* of a body of endorsements? How is one to interpret the endorsements of one´s final conclusions -- probabilities at least give one some guidance on how to *bet* on conclusions. These questions are addressed here, then continue to have a role thoughout the document. Chapter 5, on future research, raises the issues again.

Endorsements can be weighed against each other individually by pairwise-ranking criteria. For any given domain, we might establish a relevant body of endorsements and a partial ordering of endorsements. (In fact, one goal of the SOLOMON effort is to establish a small set of *general* endorsements and ranking criteria for them, so that new users of SOLOMON need not specify all endorsements from scratch.) This scheme has a powerful advantage, and two serious problems. The advantage is that a partial order of endorsements makes explicit both a basis for comparison *and* the lack of any basis for comparison. A partial order allows one to specify that A is preferred to B and C, but that no ranking exists for B and C.

Pairwise ranking of endorsements is unusual in SOLOMON, however, because the program swiftly builds up large bodies of endorsements pro and con its hypotheses. Typically, a hypothesis is supported by several reasons to believe and disbelieve the hypothesis. This research does not present a general algorithm for ranking bodies of endorsements, although an ad hoc algorithm for ranking rule endorsements is presented in section 4.3.3.1. The idea behind this algorithm is simple. Classes of endorsements, E_i, have an a priori ranking, as do endorsements e_i within each class. Statements S_i are associated with bodies of endorsements, se_i. Then, one statement, S_1, is judged to be better endorsed than another, S_2, if *both* are endorsed by members of the highest-ranking class of endorsements, if $se_1 \cap E_{best} \neq \emptyset$ and $e_2 \cap E_{best} \neq \emptyset$, *and* some endorsement $e_1 = se_1 \cap E_{best}$ ranks above $e_2 = se_2 \cap E_{best}$. If the endorsements of se_1 and se_2 do not both include members of E_{best}, then the next lowest ranked class of endorsements is found (i.e., E_{best} becomes the next-best class of endorsements), and the comparison is attempted again. This process continues until a ranking of endorsements is found for some class of endorsements, or until the system runs out of classes (in which case S_1 and S_2 are considered equally endorsed).

Bodies of endorsements are most easily ranked if a *net weight* is first derived for each. Yet, the net weight of a body of endorsements is just the conjunction of the endorsements. It is meaningless to attempt to derive a numerical weight for a body of symbolic reasons that do not themselves have any numeric interpretation. Moreover, this endeavor is antithetical to the fundamental idea of the model of endorsement -- that numeric degrees of belief should be replaced by the reasons for believing and disbelieving that they summarize. The model of endorsement is too new to but guess how the ranking issue will be resolved. My guess, however, is that meaningful combinations of endorsements will be identified, along with partial orderings of these combinations. It seems unlikely that all combinations of endorsements will be meaningful, and so the model is unlikely to need an algorithm for ranking arbitrary combinations of endorsements.

The second problem for the endorsement scheme is that of interpreting endorsements. If it is inappropriate to interpret an endorsement as a numerical weight, what interpretation should one use? Endorsements have several roles in the model of endorsement: First, as reasons for believing and disbelieving a hypothesis, they provide the information to determine whether a proposition is *certain enough* to be used in later processing. A proposition can be *adequately* or *well* endorsed, or *inadequately* or *poorly* endorsed. Adequate endorsement has the same function as finding a proposition to be true, and inadequate endorsement corresponds to finding a proposition false. However, an endorsement can be adequate for some purposes but not for others. (This clearly complicates the issue of ranking endorsements, because proposition A might more believable, i.e., have a higher-ranking endorsement, than proposition B in some contexts but not in others. This is another reason for not writing a general endorsement-ranking algorithm.) Another important role of endorsements is to guide the recovery of a problem-solving effort when it founders for lack of evidence. Endorsements record inadequacies of evidence, and are used in the model of endorsement to select an appropriate strategy for gaining more evidence, or minimizing the effects of lack of evidence. This and other roles for endorsements are discussed in 2.3.2.

A version of the problem of interpretation is, "Now I have a conclusion and its endorsements, what shall I do?" From the standpoint of the model of endorsement, a final conclusion is like any other -- it is either adequately endorsed or inadequately endorsed. Moreover, the decision is based on what the conclusion is to be used for. A recommendation that is produced by the model of endorsement should be accepted, because the criteria for its acceptance -- for judging it to be adequately endorsed -- have been specified. Said differently, provided that one states the criteria for believing a recommendation, the model of endorsement will ensure that no recommendation is made that fails to satisfy the criteria. It does, however, offer two advantages over systems that simply achieve or fail to achieve some numerical threshold for their final conclusions: First, regardless of whether a conclusion is deemed acceptable, the model can use its endorsements to explain why it is acceptable (or unacceptable). Second, if any conclusion -- including the final one -- is poorly endorsed, the model of endorsement may be able to suggest methods for discounting or resolving the residual uncertainty.

In sum, bodies of endorsements can be ranked, though endorsements and ranking criteria that are relevant to any particular domain cannot be known in advance. It would be foolish to criticize numeric approaches for not specifying in advance the degrees of belief appropriate to rules in an arbitrary domain. Similarly, the endorsement-based approach should not be criticized for not specifying the endorsements and ranking criteria that obtain for an arbitrary domain. Secondly, the endorsement-based approach is *not* designed to provide *net weights* of evidence, and should not be condemned for failing to do so. On the contrary, the goal of the approach is to break aggregate degrees of belief into their components, and to reason intelligently about the components.

2.3.5 AI Concepts Related to Endorsement

Reason maintenance. Endorsement is similar to recording justifications in a truth maintenance system (Doyle, 1979), but with a crucial difference. In the TMS, a justification is used to decide whether a conclusion has support, but the kind of support is irrelevant (see Fig. 2-3). Endorsements, however, record aspects of inferences that are relevant to reasoning about their certainty. There are many different kinds of endorsements, corresponding to different kinds of evidence for and against a proposition, and one´s confidence in a conclusion depends on its *pedigree* -- its endorsements and those of its preconditions. It is expected that individual endorsements and combinations of endorsements can be ranked (see the previous section). For example, in most contexts, eyewitness testimony is preferable to circumstantial evidence, direct evidence to indirect, corroboration to contradiction, and inference to assumption. What is meant by one kind of evidence being preferable to another is that a conclusion endorsed as having the one kind of evidence for its support is more certain than a conclusion endorsed as supported by less preferred evidence (see Fig. 2-4).

Figure 2.3: Truth-maintenance-style support for proposition B

Figure 2.4: Endorsement support for Proposition B

Sponsors. A speculative treatment of an idea similar, in some respects, to endorsement is the *sponsor* concept of Kornfeld and Hewitt´s (1981) scientific community metaphor. These authors suggest that in a system with limited resources, tasks are allocated resources by sponsors, contingent on the promise of the tasks. This idea has parallels in SOLOMON, although it doesn´t map over directly. In SOLOMON, a task is *scheduled* for execution according to its promise (see section

4.5), and tested again prior to execution to see whether it is still promising. Kornfeld and Hewitt cite as an example a test that proves very powerful in SOLOMON: They note that sponsors are unlikely to allocate resources to tasks that "attempt to establish *results already known*" (p. 29). SOLOMON, too, will not relinquish its resources to a task that is adequately endorsed for some purpose. One difference between the sponsors idea and that of endorsements is that sponsors are designed to work in a distributed system, whereas endorsements are designed for a serial SOLOMON. Another difference is that, to my knowledge, Kornfeld and Hewitt have not expanded on their original concept to differentiate the kinds and structures of sponsors, as I have done for the model of endorsement.

Human Plausible Reasoning. Allan Collins has done research on *human plausible reasoning* (1978) that has much relevance to the model of endorsement. Collins took verbal protocols from human subjects on a wide variety of not-very-certain problems, such as "whether there are black princess phones [and] when the respondent first drank beer." Collins found *certainty conditions* -- different configurations of evidence that affect certainty in characteristic ways. He also identified different inference types, especially types of *meta*-inferences, and specified characteristic certainty conditions for characteristic inference types. For example, one general meta-inference type is the *lack-of-knowledge* inference that says, essentially, "I don´t know x but I would if x were true, thus x is false." (See also the discussion of the closed-world assumption endorsements, section 4.4.1.1) Collins´ contribution was his observations of the conditions under which lack-of-knowledge and other inferences are more or less believable. For example, one´s inference that the Mekong is not a very long river is based in part on the lack-of-knowledge inference that if it were, one would know about it. The *certainty* of this inference is enhanced by the fact that one knows of several very long rivers: The Amazon, the Nile, the Mississippi, and so on. Collins noted that one can increase one´s confidence in the lack-of-knowledge inference *A lacks property B* if one knows numerous examples of things that don´t lack the property. On the other hand, one factor that works against the lack-of-knowledge inference about the length of the Mekong is that the Mekong is in a remote part of the world of which one may have little knowledge. Thus, the extent of one´s knowledge about the objects in a lack-of-knowledge inference affect the certainty of the inference. This and other cases are excellent examples of heuristic reasoning *about* uncertainty, and are intellectual forerunners of the work described in this document.

Reasons for agenda tasks: AM. Lenat´s AM program (1976) views discovery of mathematical concepts as a search in a space of concepts. The space becomes huge, and some scheduling criteria are required to determine which concepts to examine next. Ideally, only the most "interesting" concepts should be examined, and Lenat developed a set of "interestingness criteria" to associate with concepts on AM´s agenda. These are reasons to attend to the concepts; those concepts with good reasons get most attention from the system. If we view an abstract agenda as a ranked list of progressively less *believable* hypotheses, then the analogy between AM´s approach and endorsements is plain: One associates reasons for believing (and disbelieving) with hypotheses, and these are used to rank the relative credibility of hypotheses. In fact, SOLOMON uses just such an agenda of tasks (see Chapter 4, section 4.5).

Lenat recognized that the difficult part of using reasons to control attention was making them mean something to the system: "Each reason is supposed to have semantic impact on the user, and is kept around partly for that purpose" (1976, p. 40). However, the reasons for attending to tasks were not actually used by AM to allocate attention; numerical ratings were used instead. Lenat discovered, as we will find in this document, that it is difficult to use symbolic reasons for tasks that seem better suited to numerical ranking unless these reasons actually affect the behavior of the system:

> Each reason supporting a newly-suggested job is simply an English sentence (an opaque string, a token). AM cannot do much intelligent processing on these reasons. AM is not allowed to inspect parts of it,

> parse it, transform it, etc. The most AM can do is compare two such tokens for equality. Of course, it is not hard to imagine this capability extended to permit AM to syntactically analyze such strings, or to trivially compute some sort of "difference" between two given reasons. . . . Of course, *doing* [this] is . . . probably the toughest of the "open research problems" I'll propose.

3 Bayesian and Endorsement-Based Analyses: Two Cases

3.1 Introduction

The goal of this chapter is to compare the model of endorsement with probabilistic approaches to reasoning about uncertainty. To this end, two problems are given detailed analyses. The first is inspired by a very interesting paper by Shafer and Tversky (1983), in which the authors discuss several Bayesian and belief function designs for weighing evidence. The arguments they analyze are taken from a paper published in *Scientific American* (August, 1978) by Alan Walker and Richard Leakey; the paper discusses the problems caused by the uncertainty inherent in reconstructing the evolution of the hominids from fossil records. This chapter compares the Shafer-Tversky analysis of the Walker-Leakey evidence with an analysis based on the model of endorsement. The Walker-Leakey evidence also forms the basis for a second comparative analysis. This case concerns the dual role of uncertain propositions as conclusions and as evidence in later arguments. The question is how to make the credibility of conclusions sensitive to the uncertainty of their premises. A probabilistic and an endorsement-based scheme are discussed and compared.

The previous chapter illustrates that there are relatively few general approaches to dealing with uncertainty. Excluding diversification, which is really a problem solving response to uncertainty and not a representation and calculus for reasoning about uncertainty, there are just three general techniques for managing uncertainty: Ignore it, deal with it "in parallel" with domain inferences, or design a control structure that minimizes its effects. Adams (1976) writes of the several implementations of the parallel certainty inference approach (and of MYCIN's implementation in particular) that it is difficult to create "a useful and internally consistent system which is not isomorphic to a portion of probability theory." He continues

> In proposing such a system a careful delineation of its relationship to conventional probability theory can contribute to [an] understanding of and a clear exposition of its assumptions and approximations, and thereby allow tests of whether these are satisfied in the proposed field of use. (Adams, 1976, p. 185)

Although Adams advocates comparisons to the normative aspects of probability theory, while I will be comparing the representational adequacy and pragmatics of probability theory and endorsements, the purpose of this chapter is as Adams suggested: To make a comparison between probability theory and the model of endorsement that will show the fields of use in which each is an adequate and pragmatic tool.

3.2 Weighing the Evidence of Walker and Leakey

3.2.1 Introduction

Shafer and Tversky (1983) present a fascinating analysis of the number of species represented by fossil remains found in East Turkana. Their source is a paper by Walker and Leakey (1978) in *Scientific American*. Walker and Leakey discuss three distinct fossil records, and entertain five hypotheses about the number of species represented by the fossils. Shafer and Tversky discuss two *designs* -- arrangements of evidence pro and con the five hypotheses. One design is based on Bayesian theory, and the other on the theory of belief functions.

Shafer and Tversky´s concern is with what one can say about an uncertain situation, given a probability theory and a design, or arrangement, of evidence. A design is an arrangement of evidence pro and con a body of hypotheses. Implementing a design leads to an *analysis* of one´s arguments pro and con the hypotheses. It is the properties of these analyses that concern Shafer and Tversky.

They are concerned with the *epistemological adequacy* (McCarthy, 1968) of the Bayesian and belief function theories, with the facility of these theories to express arguments about evidence. Shafer and Tversky, in fact, view the two theories as languages:

> A theory of probability is very much like a language. At its base is a vocabulary -- a scale of degrees of probability. Attached to this vocabulary is a semantics -- a scale of canonical examples that show how the vocabulary is to be interpreted and psychological devices for making the interpretation effective as a means of matching real problems to the scale. And elements of the vocabulary are combined according to a syntax -- the theory´s calculus. (pp. 4-5)

The authors note that the acceptability of designs -- arrangements of evidence -- depends, at base, on the quantities they require us to assess: "Often one design is superior to another simply because the questions it asks can be answered with greater confidence and precision." Thus, in considering a design for the Walker-Leakey analysis, they consider which questions they might ask of Walker and Leakey so that they will be satisfied with the precision and credibility of the answers. For example, they note that for this problem, likelihood ratios[1] may be more confidently assessed than absolute probabilities:

> We can think about how much less likely the observed disparity among the three groups would be if they represented fewer than three species, but we would be totally at sea if asked to assess the unconditional chance of this degree of disparity among three extinct hominid species.

---

[1] A likelihood ratio has the form $P(e|H_0)/P(e|H_1)$. It is the ratio of the likelihood of observing evidence e given hypothesis H_0, to the likelihood of observing evidence e given hypothesis H_1.

3.2.2 The Problem of the Three Fossil Forms

The problem for Walker and Leakey is whether fossils, found east of Lake Turkana, in Kenya, represent one, two, or three species. The fossils are named and described as follows:

1. *Robust*. A form with very large jaws and molar and premolar teeth, wide-fanning cheekbones, and a cranial capacity of about 500 cubic centimeters. This form has also been found in South Africa and East Asia. Experts seem satisfied to classify this form as a species, *Australopithecus robustus*.

2. *Gracile*. A smaller form than *robustus*, but with similar cranial capacity and slightly smaller molars and premolars. This form lacks the wide-flaring cheekbones.

3. *Erectus*. A form identified with *Homo Erectus* specimens found in the Far East, namely, Java and northern China. This form has a small jaw and a large cranial capacity, averaging 850 cubic centimeters.

Walker and Leakey report that these records from East Turkana are contemporaneous with each other. They discuss five hypotheses about how many species the records represent. The *single-species hypothesis*, which is discussed at length here, is that all the fossils represent the same species. This hypothesis is be abbreviated $\mathbf{H1_{R\&G\&E}}$ There are three *two-species hypotheses*: One is that the *robustus* and *gracile* forms are male and female of the same species while the *erectus* form is of a second species; this is abbreviated $\mathbf{H2_{E,R\&G}}$. Another is that the *robustus* form is a species and the *gracile* and *erectus* forms are female and male members of a second species; this is abbreviated $\mathbf{H3_{R,G\&E}}$. The third two-species hypothesis is that the *gracile* form is its own species, and the other two forms belong to a second species; abbreviated $\mathbf{H4_{G,R\&E}}$ Finally, there is the *three-species hypothesis* that each form represents a distinct species. This is abbreviated $\mathbf{H5_{R,G,E}}$. These hypotheses are summarized in Table 3-1.

1. The three forms are all members of a single species ($H1_{R\&G\&E}$).

2. Two species, of which *robustus* and *gracile* are male and female forms of *Australopithecus robustus*, and the large-brained form represents *Homo erectus* ($H2_{E,R\&G}$).

3. Two species, of which one is represented by the *robustus* form and the other is represented by the *erectus* form and the *gracile* form as male and female, respectively ($H3_{R,G\&E}$).

4. Two species, of which one is the *gracile* form and the other is represented by the admittedly variable *robustus* and *erectus* forms ($H4_{G,R\&E}$).

5. The three forms represent three species ($H5_{R,G,E}$).

Table 3.1: Walker and Leakey´s Hypotheses.

The evidence for the single-species hypothesis ($\mathbf{H1_{R\&G\&E}}$) is the theoretical argument that once a hominid species acquires culture, its ecological niche expands very rapidly and it crowds out other species, particularly hominid species without culture. By this argument, there cannot be two distinct hominid species with culture. The evidence against this hypothesis and against $\mathbf{H4_{G,R\&E}}$ is that the *robustus* and *erectus* have evolved *opposite* adaptations: The former has big teeth and a little brain, and the latter has the opposite characteristics. Evidence against the second and third hypotheses is that they require sexual dimorphism in excess of any known in living hominid populations. Furthermore, it is noted that while *erectus* fossils have been found in China and Java, *gracile* and *robustus* fossils have not. This is contrary to hypotheses $\mathbf{H3_{R,G\&E}}$ and $\mathbf{H_{G,R\&E}}$. This evidence is summarized in Table 3-2.

It is interesting to note that before the *erectus* form was found in East Turkana, Walker and Leakey favored the hypothesis that the *robustus* and *gracile* forms were members of the same species. When they wrote their paper in 1978, however, they favored hypothesis $\mathbf{H5_{G,R,E}}$, above.

1. Pro hypothesis $H1_{R\&G\&E}$: The general theoretical argument that distinct hominid species cannot coexist after one of them has acquired culture.

2. Con hypotheses $H1_{R\&G\&E}$, $H3_{R,G\&E}$ and $H4_{G,R\&E}$: Markedly different adaptations *within* a hypothetical species. The *erectus* form has a significantly larger cranial capacity and significantly smaller teeth and jaws than the other forms.

3. Con hypotheses $H1_{R\&G\&E}$, $H2_{E,R\&G}$ and $H3_{R,G\&E}$: Significant sexual dimorphism. The degree of sexual dimorphism required for hypothesis $H2_{E,R\&G}$ is possible, but the cranial capacity differences required for hypothesis $H3_{R,G\&E}$ seems much less plausible.

4. Con hypotheses $H1_{R\&G\&E}$, $H2_{E,R\&G}$. The *erectus* form is abundant in Java and northern China, but the *robustus* form is absent. It seems unlikely, then that *robustus* and the *erectus* forms are members of the same species.

5. Con hypotheses $H1_{R\&G\&E}$, $H3_{R,G\&E}$. Similarly, the *gracile* form is absent from the Far East, so it is unlikely that the *gracile* and *erectus* forms are of the same species.

Table 3.2: Evidence for Walker and Leakey´s Evidence

First, I will present Walker and Leakey´s qualitative assessment of their evidence for each of their five hypotheses. Although they talk about assessing the probabilities of the hypotheses, they do not do so. Shafer and Tversky, however, discuss a design or arrangement of the evidence that seems to capture Walker and Leakey´s reasoning. It requires that probabilities be assessed if the Bayesian calculus is to produce final probabilities for each hypothesis, but Shafer and Tversky regard this as something of a detail. The important issue is whether their design, which I will discuss, represents the reasoning of Walker and Leakey. Next, I will present an analysis of the Walker and Leakey arguments in the language of endorsements; and, finally, I will compare the approaches.

3.2.3 Walker and Leakey´s Arguments

Walker and Leakey present one argument for and two arguments against the single-species hypotheses (**$H1_{R\&G\&E}$**). (All quotations are from pages 65 and 66 of their Scientific American article, unless otherwise noted.)

> Once culture became the human domain -- and evidence for this can be sought in the fossil bones by looking for basic human anatomical attributes that developed along with culture -- the human ecological niche became so large that the species with culture always had the edge over any other species in competition for the available resources.

> We think the probability that the single-species hypothesis is correct is very low. First, the hypothesis involves accepting the fact that there is an enormous amount of intraspecies variability. Second, we think, along with others, that the adaptations apparent in the skulls of both extreme forms (*Homo erectus* and *Australopithecus robustus*) are different. In *H. erectus* the size of the brain case seems to overwhelm the chewing apparatus, as it does in living man. In *A. robustus* the opposite is true.

The first argument is without explicit support; it may be commonplace among physical anthropologists that one does not find such intraspecies variability or, the support may come from implicit reference to living populations. We simply don´t know. The second argument is apparently that a single species does not adapt in two different directions. This argument is implicit, though there is explicit mention of corroboration among colleagues that *H. erectus* and *A. robustus* exhibit different adaptations.

Note that the *gracile* form is not considered as evidence against the single-species hypothesis (**$H1_{R\&G\&E}$**). It might well have been, since its dentition is somewhat different from that of *A. robustus*, and its cranial capacity is markedly different from that of *H. erectus*.

Walker and Leakey invoke the same arguments against hypothesis $H4_{G,R\&E}$ as they used against the first, namely, that *A. robustus* and *H. erectus* cannot exhibit such different physical characteristics and still be part of the same species. In addition, they marshal evidence about the geographical distribution of similar remains:

> One must also ask why no specimens of *A. robustus* are found in Java and China, where *H. erectus* specimens are comparatively abundant. If the answer is that such specimens were present, but for some reason were not fossilized or have not yet been unearthed, then how is it that *A. robustus* is the commonest hominid in the East African fossil record?

The first argument is that if *A. robustus* and *H. erectus were* of the same species, then they should both have been found in Java and China. Note, in addition, the anticipatory argument against the possibility that *A. robustus does* exist in Java and China, but has yet to be found. This is an important argument, considering the authors' own trepidation that the number of fossil remains is in any case small. They counter the problem of an absolute and small sample by reasoning about relative frequencies *within* the sample, saying that *A. robustus* is by far the most frequent find in East Africa, so it seems unlikely that it should be completely absent in China and Java. They even present a *causal argument* of why the *A. robustus* form should be more in evidence than the other forms in East Africa, noting that the relative abundance of the massive jaws and teeth of *A. robustus* in the East Turkana sediments "probably results more from their mechanical strength and thus their enhanced ability to survive fossilization, than from any preponderance of *A. robustus* individuals in the population" (p. 60).

Note the slight inconsistency in the arguments: The first argument is that if *A. robustus* and *H. erectus* were of the same species, then their *populations* and thus numbers of *fossil remains* would be similar in Java and China to those in East Africa. However, the causal argument above suggests that the numerosity of fossil remains may not be a strong indicator of population sizes. Thus, the absence of fossil remains of *A. robustus* in China and Java is not *necessarily* an argument that it did not roam with *H. erectus*. While the first argument relies on a correspondence between populations and fossil remains, the second argument questions whether such correspondences can be inferred. There is no indication that Walker and Leakey are aware of this inconsistency, which is a testament to the remarkable and necessary ability to form coherent arguments in the face of slight discrepancies.[2] Walker and Leakey´s third hypothesis (**$H3_{R,G\&E}$**) is that *A. robustus* is a distinct species, while the *gracile* form and *H. erectus* are female and male representatives of the same species, respectively. The degree of sexual dimorphism with respect to cranial capacity disturbs the authors, but the addition of a second argument against the hypothesis seems to provide a clincher:

> It would be difficult enough to account for the enormous dimorphism in brain size without having to supply an answer to an additional question: Why are these gracile forms of *Australopithecus* not found as fossils in Java and China?

Hypotheses 1 through 4 have been discarded, leaving hypothesis 5 (**$H5_{G,R,E}$**) regnant. Walker and Leakey note "Sorted out this way, none of the specimens within each group shows more variability in brain size and chewing apparatus than we see among living anthropoids."

Note that in their analysis, Walker and Leakey present very little evidence *for* any hypothesis except the first. This certainly simplifies the analysis, since the authors are then relieved of resolving conflicting evidence. It seems characteristic of Walker and Leakey´s arguments (and possibly of physical anthropology

[2] The second analysis, however, illustrates more glaring inconsistency.

arguments in general) to believe something unless reason is discovered to disbelieve it. They note, for example, that until the first large-brained *H. erectus* fossil was found, they were quite willing to believe that the ***robustus*** and ***gracile*** forms were male and female of the same species.

3.2.4 A Shafer-Tversky Analysis of the Walker-Leakey Evidence

Shafer and Tversky propose two designs, or arrangements of evidence, pro and con the five hypotheses of Walker and Leakey. One design is based on Bayesian theory, and one on the theory of belief functions. I shall only discuss the Bayesian design. (See section 2.2.5 for a general discussion of belief functions.)

The issue raised by Shafer and Tversky is not, of course, how many species are represented by the fossil remains at East Turkana, but whether the Bayesian language adequately represents the evidential reasoning of Walker and Leakey. I have a similar concern for the model of endorsement. Thus, we "change tracks" here from a discussion of the evidence itself to a discussion of what *kind* of evidence it is, and how the evidence is to be organized in an analysis of arguments.

We will use Shafer and Tversky´s notation -- the numbers **i, ii , . . . , v** -- for the five arguments introduced by Walker and Leakey as evidence for and against their five hypotheses. These hypotheses are denoted $\mathbf{H1}_{\mathbf{R\&G\&E}}$, $\mathbf{H2}_{\mathbf{E,R\&G}}$, $\mathbf{H3}_{\mathbf{R,G\&E}}$, $\mathbf{H4}_{\mathbf{G,R\&E}}$, and $\mathbf{H5}_{\mathbf{G,R,E}}$ as before. (For reference, see Tables 3-1 and 3-2.)

Shafer and Tversky first review a number of Bayesian designs and the criteria for using them. They settle on a *partitioning design*:

> In partitioning designs we begin our process of probability judgement with all our evidence in hand, but we deliberately partition this evidence into "old evidence" and "new evidence," assess probabilities

> on the basis of the old evidence alone, and then condition on the new evidence. (p. 40)
>
> Which of the items of evidence shall we classify as old evidence, and which as new? The obvious move is to classify (i) as old evidence and to treat (ii)-(v) as our new evidence A. (p. 45)

The intention of Shafer and Tversky is to use Bayes´s theorem to derive $P(H_i|A)$, that is, the probability of each hypothesis H_i conditioned on the "new" evidence A. The reason they call their design a partitioning design is that the prior probabilities $P(\mathbf{H1}_{\mathbf{R\&G\&E}}),...,P(\mathbf{H5}_{\mathbf{G,R,E}})$ are to be assessed on the basis of the "old" evidence, (i). A further elaboration of the design is had by further partitioning the new evidence, A, into two independent arguments: A_1 is the evidence of morphological differences (i.e., cranial size and dentition, items (ii) and (iii)); and A_2 is the evidence that the *gracile* and *robustus* forms are not found with the *erectus* form in China and Java (items (iv) and (v)). Since A_1 and A_2 are assumed to be conditionally independent $P(A \mid H_i) = P(A_1 \mid H_i)P(A_2 \mid H_i)$.

Bayes´ theorem states

$$P(H_i \mid A) = \frac{P(H_i)P(A \mid H_i)}{\Sigma P(H_j)P(A \mid H_j)} \tag{3.1}$$

Thus, for the Walker-Leakey analysis, Shafer and Tversky must assess the prior probabilities $P(H_j)$, and the conditional probabilities $P(A \mid H_j)$, for all hypotheses j, from which the denominator of (3.1) can be constructed. In general, this data requirement is unrealistic (see section 2.2.4), although it is probably manageable for this simple problem. Shafer and Tversky note, however, that the expression for $P(H_i \mid A)$ can be divided by the expression for $P(H_j \mid A)$, which gives

$$\frac{P(H_i \mid A)}{P(H_j \mid A)} = \frac{P(H_i)\ P(A \mid H_i)}{P(H_j)\ P(A \mid H_j)}$$

or

$$\frac{P(H_i \mid A)}{P(H_j \mid A)} = \frac{P(H_i)}{P(H_j)} L(A \mid H_i{:}H_j) \tag{3.2}$$

$L(A \mid H_i{:}H_j) = P(A \mid H_i)/P(A \mid H_j)$ is called the *likelihood ratio* favoring H_i over H_j (Shafer and Tversky, p. 46). With this reformulation, Shafer and Tversky need no longer assess the probabilities required by (3.1), but can now assess just the priors $P(H_i)$, and the likelihood ratios $L(A \mid H_i{:}H_j)$. (This appproach is used in the Prospector program. See Duda, Hart, and Nillson, 1976). They extend this design to the two pieces of evidence A_1 and A_2, but the details need not concern us here.

Next, Shafer and Tversky "assess" -- by supposition, since Walker and Leakey do not provide these data in their article -- the prior probabilities $P(H_i)$. A problem with their design, and of the Bayesian language in general, arises. The old evidence (i) supports the single-species hypothesis ($\mathbf{H1_{R\&G\&E}}$), and Shafer and Tversky assign $P(\mathbf{H1_{R\&G\&E}}) = .75$. But the evidence does not favor the other hypotheses, so there is no guidance as to how to divide up the remaining .25 of the total distribution among the other hypotheses. On the basis of some arguments made by Walker and Leaky, Shafer and Tversky adopt the scheme shown in the first column of Table 3-3.

After the prior probabilities, Shafer and Tversky assess the likelihood ratios $L(A_1 \mid \mathbf{H_i{:}H5_{G,R,E}})$ and $L(A_2 \mid \mathbf{H_i{:}H5_{G,R,E}})$:

> Now, consider A_1, the argument that the different types must represent three distinct species because of their [morphological] diversity. The design asks us, in effect, to assess how much less likely this diversity would be under the the one-species hypothesis and under the various two-species hypotheses. (p. 49)

These ratios are shown in Table 3-3. It is important to note that Walker and Leakey´s speculations about the likelihoods of the various two-species hypotheses are reflected in these numbers. For example, Walker and Leakey write "The second hypothesis, we think, is is more likely to be correct than the third," and, indeed, it is represented as ten times more likely in Table 3-3.

Evidence of the absence of *robustus* and *gracile* forms from China and Java is considered in the third column of Table 3-3. Again, the question that the design asks one to assess is how much less likely it is that these forms should be absent under the one- and two-species hypotheses than under the three-species hypothesis. Shafer and Tversky take .01 as a reasonable likelihood ratio; they ascribe to Walker and Leakey the belief that the absence of *robustus* and *gracile* forms from China and Java is a hundred times less likely if they are members of the same species as *H. erectus* than if they are not.

The last column in Table 3-3 shows the derived probabilities of the five original hypotheses conditioned on the evidence. Shafer and Tversky´s hypothetical assessments result in an analysis that agrees with Walker and Leakey´s own.

	$P(H_i)$	$L(A_1 \mid H_i{:}H5_{G,R,E})$	$L(A_2 \mid H_i{:}H5_{G,R,E})$	$P(H_i \mid A)$
$H1_{R\&G\&E}$	.75	.01	.01	.00060
$H2_{E,R\&G}$	.05	.50	1.00	.19983
$H3_{R,G\&E}$	.05	.05	.01	.00020
$H4_{G,R\&E}$	.05	.01	.01	.00004
$H5_{G,R,E}$	.10	1.00	1.00	.79933

Table 3.3: Shafer and Tversky´s analysis of the Walker-Leakey arguments.

Let us summarize the intent and process of Shafer and Tversky´s analysis. Their goal was to show that their probability language and design are sufficient to represent the evidential reasoning of Walker and Leakey. Their underlying thesis is that a good design is one that requires meaningful data, and they demonstrated this with the contrast between assessing likelihood ratios and assessing absolute probabilities. Shafer and Tversky's analysis involved a partitioning design, in which the old evidence was the theoretical argument that distinct hominid species cannot coexist if one species has culture. Prior probabilities of each of Walker and Leakey's five hypotheses were assessed on the basis of this evidence. The new evidence for the analysis was A_1, the morphological differences between the three forms, and A_2, the disproportionate geographic distribution of the forms. Bayes's theorem requires a lot of data, but Shafer and Tversky show how a design can be achieved that requires only the prior probabilities and likelihood ratios. Thus, they develop a design that is mathematically simple; and that requires meaningful, and relatively little, data. Lastly, Shafer and Tversky make up numbers to plug into their design. The authors note that it is not their proper role to assess these numbers, that that is a task for the experts. But, of course, the numbers Shafer and Tversky use are largely irrelevant, since their goal is to show the representational adequacy of their language and design.

3.2.5 An Endorsement-based Analysis of Walker and Leakey's Evidence

The major class of endorsements, as we shall see in Chapter 4, pertains to inference rules. The evidence of Walker and Leakey is not represented in the form of inference rules, but it can very easily be recast in that form. Figure 3-1 illustrates the division of the evidence that Shafer and Tversky used in their analysis. The notation of these rules is explained in Section 2.3.3.1.

The first rule in Figure 3-1 simply rephrases as a conditional the argument that a hominid species that lacks culture cannot coexist with one that has obtained culture, and the latter will dominate. This theoretical argument was used as evidence for Walker and Leakey's hypothesis 1 ($\mathbf{H1_{R\&G\&E}}$), that the three fossil forms represented a single species. The interpretation of rule 1 is "If ?form-1 is a hominid form, and ?form-2 is a hominid form, and the population represented by form-1 had culture, then ?form-1 and ?form-2 must be of the same species." This crude representation of the argument leaves out many subleties, such as whether ?form-1 and ?form-2 were contemporaries; nonetheless, it suffices for this example.

The second rule in Figure 3-1 collapses a great deal of Walker and Leakey's reasoning into a single argument about morphology, and in so doing, loses much of the force of their argument. Rule 2 says "If ?form-1 and ?form-2 have different morphology, then they are of different species." As we saw above, Walker and Leakey used arguments about the plausibility of degree of sexual dimorphism and the plausibility of opposite adaptations within a species. I have reduced these to a single "morphology" rule to make this analysis directly comparable to that of Shafer and Tversky; later I will discuss the problems this causes and expand the analysis.

Rule 3 in Figure 3-1 says "If you find a form at a place and not at another place, then the forms are not of the same species." Again, this rule lacks some subtleties such as delimiting the geographical size of **place** and the time at which the forms occupied the place, but it will work for **place** = **(China and Java)**, assuming that the forms were contemporaries. (In the absurd extreme, we might use the rule to claim that since no two objects can occupy the same space at the same time, any two objects can be shown to be of different species.)

Before continuing with the analysis, I want to note some potential confusion in the use of the words "evidence" and "argument." My personal inclination is to regard propositions such as "the *gracile* form has a cranial capacity of 500 c.c." as evidence, and the statement "the *gracile* form cannot be of the same species as the *erectus* form because their morphologies are different" as an argument. Thus, an inference rule captures an argument. An inference rule asserts a conclusion -- which may subsequently be used as evidence -- when evidence is found to satisfy the rule's condition.

```
(if (and (hominid ?form-1)
         (hominid ?form-2)
         (not-equal ?form-1 ?form-2)
         (have-culture ?form-1))
 then (single-species ?form-1 ?form-2))

(if (different-morphology ?form-1 ?form-2)
 then (different-species ?form-1 ?form-2))

(if (and (found-at ?place-1 ?form-1)
         (not (found-at ?place-1 ?form-2))
 then (different-species ?form-1 ?form-2))
```

Figure 3.1: Three rules corresponding to the Shafer-Tversky partition of Walker and Leakey´s evidence

Now consider Walker and Leakey´s first hypothesis, that the *A. robustus*, *gracile*, and *H. erectus* fossils represent a single species. Further consider, for simplicity, that the single species hypothesis is tested by asking whether it holds for *H. erectus* and *A. robustus*. This is the test made by Walker and Leakey, and is only one of several possible. If *H. erectus* and *A. robustus* are both hominid forms, and it may be assumed that one had culture, then the forms must be of the same species. This is the import of rule 1 in Figure 3.1. Interestingly, Walker and Leakey do not say whether they have evidence of culture in *H. erectus*, only that both had "human characteristics" and that they "nominate *Australopithecus* for the role of the hominid without culture." For the sake of the example, though, let us assume that they claim culture for *H. erectus*, and assert that it and *Australopithecus* must have been the same species.[3] Similarly, the evidence of Walker and Leakey

[3] The other tack would still allow us evidence of a weaker kind for the single-species hypothesis: We could claim the *potential* of evidence for the hypothesis, contingent on the evidence of culture in *H. erectus*. It may be a common and labor-saving mode of inference to say a result is contingent on evidence that we can´t afford to produce, but let us believe the result anyway. It is certainly a common mode of inference to say that a result will be believed unless there is evidence to the contrary.

satisfies the conditions of rules 2 and 3 in Figure 3.1 – *H. erectus* and *A. robustus* do have different morphology, and *H. erectus* is found in Java (and China) while *A. robustus* is not -- so the conclusions of these rules can be asserted.

Given these three conclusions, based on evidence, we now engage in an analysis of arguments, developing an arrangement of the evidence, as Shafer and Tversky do. Recall that the two steps in analyzing arguments in the model of endorsement are to decide which column of the ledger-book an argument belongs in, and to do the "accounting" of arguments (see section 2.3.1). The computational mechanism for the first step is discussed in section 4.4.1.3, but we can see that the conclusion of the first rule in Figure 3.1 supports the single-species hypothesis, while the other two argue against it. This is shown in Figure 3.2.

Evidence pro	Evidence con
(**single-species** *H. erectus* *A. robustus*)	(**different-species** *H. erectus* *A. robustus*)
	(**different-species** *H. erectus* *A. robustus*)

Figure 3.2: Ledger-book for Single-Species Hypothesis

The next step in the analysis is to perform the accounting: Do the two arguments in the *Evidence con* column outweigh the argument in the *Evidence pro* column? Although Walker and Leakey agree that they do, the question is generally difficult to answer. The accounting must depend, in general, on the *quality* and the *kind* of the evidence. The quality of the evidence of different morphology is very high: There is no dispute that three *forms* are under discussion, and those of *A. robustus* and *H. erectus* could not be mistaken for each other by a trained physical anthropologist. However, we should note that the quality of evidence *produced* by rule 2 in Figure 3-1 -- the conclusion of that rule -- may not be entirely trustworthy. Recall, for example, that the *gracile* and *robustus* forms were known to have different morphologies but *were* considered members of the same species by Walker and Leakey until *H. erectus* was discovered. Thus, the inference that different morphologies imply different species is too general, and we should be circumspect about all conclusions of the inference. As with the premise of rule 2, the quality of the evidence for the premise of rule 3 is good: *H. erectus* is found in Java and China where *A. robustus* is not. However, we should note some consternation that the conclusion of the rule is based on having *not* found something. In general, this *kind* of conclusion requires some other information to make it believable; for example, we want to be assured that Walker and Leakey (or their colleagues) have looked for *A. robustus* in Java and China, and that they would have found it if it existed, before we accept their inability to find *A. robustus* as evidence.

The accounting of arguments for and against the single species hypothesis is, thus, not a simple polling process. We do not have a "one argument, one vote" setup, but rather, an accounting in which the credibility of the arguments determines their relative weight. We have seen that there are good reasons to mistrust, or at least scrutinize, the conclusions of rules 2 and 3. The first such qualification was introduced as an artifact of constructing rule 2: The rule is too general. The second qualification was implicit in Walker and Leakey´s own reasoning: They posit, as does rule 3, a conclusion based on the absence of evidence.

If arguments for and against a hypothesis do not carry equal weight, then we need some representation of the weight they do carry. In the model of endorsement, this is provided by explicit records of the *reasons* -- called endorsements -- for believing and disbelieving an argument. Figure 3-3 shows the ledger-book for the single-species hypotheses with the endorsements discussed above in place.[4] Note that the accounting process must now be qualitative instead of quantitative: We must ask whether the argument for the single-species hypothesis is sufficiently well-endorsed to outweigh the arguments against the hypothesis.

Similar ledger-book arrangements can be constructed for Walker and Leakey´s other hypotheses. The second, third, and fourth hypotheses have no evidence to support them and the conclusions of rules 2 and 3 against them. We will return to a more detailed consideration of these arguments, shortly, but first we will examine the basis for accepting Walker and Leakey´s fifth hypothesis.

<u>Evidence pro</u>

(single-species *H. erectus, A. robustus*)
endorsements:
1. From rule 1, Fig. 3.1:
2. A theoretical tenet, unproved and perhaps unprovable.

<u>Evidence con</u>

(different-species *H. erectus, A. robustus*)
endorsements:
1. From rule 2, Fig. 3.1
2. Premise is highly believable
3. Conclusion is too general

(different-species *H. erectus A. robustus*)
endorsements:
1. From rule 3, Fig. 3.1
2. Conclusion is based on absence of evidence

Figure 3.3: Ledger-book for Single-Species Hypothesis

Walker and Leakey´s fifth hypothesis is that the *robustus*, *gracile*, and *erectus* forms represent three different species. They accept the hypothesis on the basis of two kinds of arguments: First, the interpretation is consistent with what is known

[4] Actually, the "endorsements" in Figure 3-3 are just mnemonics to remind us of the arguments of the previous paragraphs. The actual structure of endorsements is discussed in Chapter 4.

about living primates and, second, there is evidence to reject the other hypotheses:

> The hypothesis with the best chance of being correct, we believe, is the last of the five: that three species are present. Sorted out this way, none of the specimens within each group shows more variability in brain size and chewing apparatus than we see among living anthropoids.

Shafer and Tversky do not account for the comparison to living anthropoids in their analysis, and so there are no rules in 3-1 to represent this argument. We will delete it from this analysis to maintain consistency with Shafer and Tversky, and also because it seems to lend relatively little weight to the analysis. For example, Walker and Leakey believed a two-species hypothesis, despite the implied "variability in brain size and chewing apparatus," until the H. *erectus* fossils were found. Thus, it seems to be the kind of argument that one throws in for support but ignores when it runs contrary to one´s current hypothesis (see the discussion of *supportive* endorsements, Section 4.4.1.1).

There is a variety of ways to construct a ledger-book for the fifth hypothesis. One simple example is shown in Figure 3-4. The point to note about it is that the evidence for the hypothesis is an argument about other hypotheses. In particular, there is an implied exhaustiveness of the five hypotheses that allows Walker and Leakey to conclude the fifth from disproof of the first four. It is worth recording this assumption as an endorsement. It provides a natural basis for doubting the three-species hypothesis should other fossil remains be unearthed and result in additional hypotheses about the current three forms. This is exactly what happened, recall, when the *H. erectus* fossils were found. Prior to that time, Walker and Leakey entertained just the hypotheses that the *gracile* and *robustus* forms were a) of the same species, or b) of different species. They concluded the former because there was inadequate evidence for the latter. In the ledger-book formalism, this conclusion would accrue an endorsement noting the assumed exhaustiveness of the two hypotheses, so that when the third fossil form was discovered and the corpus of hypotheses was expanded, the original conclusion would become suspect.

Evidence pro	Evidence con
(different species *A. robustus, gracile, H. erectus***)** **endorsements:** 1. From ledger-books 1, 2, 3, and 4 and the assumption that the five hypotheses are exhaustive	

Figure 3.4: Ledger-book for Three-Species Hypothesis

3.3 Comparison of the Bayesian and Endorsement-based Approaches

In this section Shafer and Tversky's analysis of the Walker-Leakey evidence will be compared with the endorsement-based analysis of the last section. We will compare the analyses along the dimensions of *representational adequacy* and *the ease of constructing the analyses*. Evaluation of the approaches along the first dimension involves asking "What can I say about uncertainty in the language of Bayesian theory and the language of endorsements." Evaluation along the second dimension involves a specialization of the first question: "What kinds of statements about uncertainty are especially easy or especially difficult to make in the language of each approach."

A failure of the endorsement-based analysis is that it does not easily capture Walker and Leakey's statement that "The second hypothesis, we think, is more likely to be correct than the third" (p. 66). Figures 3-5 and 3-6 show the evidence pro and con each of these hypotheses. We can see that each hypothesis must be rejected because it lacks any positive evidence but is damned by negative evidence. What we lack is a representation of *degree* of belief that will immediately show that the evidence against the third hypothesis, $\mathbf{H3}_{\mathbf{R,G\&E}}$, is more damaging than that against the second, $\mathbf{H2}_{\mathbf{E,R\&G}}$.

Evidence pro	Evidence con
	(different-species *A. robustus, gracile***)** **endorsements:** 1. From rule 2, Fig. 3.1

Figure 3.5: Ledger-book for Hypothesis 2

(Note that Figs. 3-5 and 3-6 do not include the endorsements of evidence shown in Fig. 3-3. These endorsements may indeed have played a role in Walker and Leakey's preference for $\mathbf{H2}_{\mathbf{E,R\&G}}$ over $\mathbf{H3}_{\mathbf{R,G\&E}}$. However, there is no evidence in their paper that this is the case, and so the endorsements, having served their pedagogical purpose, have been dropped.)

However, we should note that there is some ambiguity in Walker and Leakey's analysis about *why* the second hypothesis ($\mathbf{H2}_{\mathbf{E,R\&G}}$) is preferred to the third ($\mathbf{H3}_{\mathbf{R,G\&E}}$). One argument is that $\mathbf{H2}_{\mathbf{E,R\&G}}$ implies less sexual dimorphism than $\mathbf{H3}_{\mathbf{R,G\&E}}$; another is that while $\mathbf{H2}_{\mathbf{E,R\&G}}$ is damaged by the sexual dimorphism evidence, $\mathbf{H3}_{\mathbf{R,G\&E}}$ is damaged by this evidence *and* the geographic distribution evidence (argument 5 from Table 3-2). The endorsement-based approach captures the latter argument easily: Figure 3-6 can be seen to bring two pieces of evidence to bear against its hypothesis, while Figure 3-5 admits just one negative argument. This pooling of negative evidence results in an endorsement of *corroboration* between the pieces of evidence in Figure 3-6. We can easily say that the converse of $\mathbf{H3}_{\mathbf{R,G\&E}}$ is more highly believed than the converse of $\mathbf{H2}_{\mathbf{E,R\&G}}$,

because the former is endorsed by corroborating evidence. But the endorsement-based approach does not easily capture the first argument, that $\mathbf{H2}_{\mathbf{E,R\&G}}$ is preferred to $\mathbf{H3}_{\mathbf{R,G\&E}}$ because it involves *less* of something unlikely, namely, sexual dimorphism, than does $\mathbf{H3}_{\mathbf{R,G\&E}}$. This kind of argument is easily made in the Bayesian approach, since it is a probability argument.

Evidence pro	Evidence con
	(different-species *H. erectus, gracile***)** **endorsements:** 1. From rule 2, Fig. 3.1 2. Corroboration between this argument and the subsequent one.
	(different-species *H. erectus A. robustus***)** **endorsements:** 1. From rule 3, Fig. 3.1 2. Corroboration between this argument and the previous one.

Figure 3.6: Ledger-book for Hypothesis 3

A possibility that we must consider is that $\mathbf{H2}_{\mathbf{E,R\&G}}$ is preferred to $\mathbf{H3}_{\mathbf{R,G\&E}}$ by Walker and Leakey both because of the superior likelihood of the degree of dimorphism implied by $\mathbf{H2}_{\mathbf{E,R\&G}}$ and because $\mathbf{H3}_{\mathbf{R,G\&E}}$ is more completely damned by contrary evidence, but that the relative weight of these arguments is not explicit. In this case, the endorsement-based approach will still show that $\mathbf{H2}_{\mathbf{E,R\&G}}$ is preferred to $\mathbf{H3}_{\mathbf{R,G\&E}}$, but only because of a lucky arrangement of evidence! Imagine that endorsements for the conclusion of rule 2 (in Fig. 3-1) have been constructed to represent the degree of sexual dimorphism as a factor affecting one´s belief: The endorsement **low degree of sexual dimorphism** is a weak reason to disbelieve its associated hypothesis, while the endorsement **high degree of sexual dimorphism** is a much stronger reason for disbelief. Then regardless of the relative weight of the two pieces of evidence, $\mathbf{H2}_{\mathbf{E,R\&G}}$ will be preferred to $\mathbf{H3}_{\mathbf{R,G\&E}}$. This is true because the corroboration endorsement arises in the analysis of $\mathbf{H3}_{\mathbf{R,G\&E}}$, where the implied degree of sexual dimorphism is greatest. In a less fortuitous arrangement of evidence, it might be difficult to decide which of $\mathbf{H2}_{\mathbf{E,R\&G}}$ and $\mathbf{H3}_{\mathbf{R,G\&E}}$ was preferred. For example, if the sexual dimorphism implied by $\mathbf{H2}_{\mathbf{E,R\&G}}$ was *more* than that implied by $\mathbf{H3}_{\mathbf{R,G\&E}}$, then we would have to ask "$\mathbf{H2}_{\mathbf{E,R\&G}}$ is condemned by the extreme improbability of a high degree of sexual dimorphism, while $\mathbf{H3}_{\mathbf{R,G\&E}}$ is condemned by the slight probability of a low degree of sexual dimorphism, and by the corroboration of this argument with the geographic argument of rule 3 (Fig. 3-1). Which hypothesis is preferred?"

Given this last example, we can see that an inability or unwillingness to specify the relative weight of endorsements can limit the usefulness of the endorsement-based approach. (Indeed, an *inability* to state any endorsements for a domain suggests that the endorsement-based approach is inappropriate for the domain.) Probability theory has a clear advantage over the model of endorsement in such cases, because it allows a respondent to say "The evidence for A is more compelling than the evidence for B, but I cannot or will not explain why this is the case." In such cases we can ask the respondent for absolute probabilities of A and B given the evidence for each, or follow Shafer and Tversky´s lead and ask for a likelihood ratio of these probabilities. Although this speaks well for the ease of representing arguments about uncertainty with probabilities, this facility comes at a price. In effect, it lets our respondent off the hook, it lets him get away with stating beliefs without justifications, and it leads to the necessary assumption that degrees of belief are entire, and comparable without further consideration. Stating a degree of belief without recounting its mental construction thus has advantages and disadvantages. But failing to obtain endorsements also has disadvantages. Quite possibly, a hybrid approach of asking for both endorsements and numbers will prove most satisfactory.

One representational advantage of the model of endorsement is that it makes different *kinds* of endorsement explicit. This is explained fully in Chapter 4, but for now, consider the endorsements introduced in this chapter. Rule 2 in Figure 3-1 was endorsed as *too general*, because it leads to the conclusion of different speciation in one case where the experts (Walker and Leakey) originally thought speciation was the same. This kind of endorsement is called a *rule endorsement*, specifically an endorsement of the rule´s condition. Similarly, rule 3 in Figure 3-1 involved inference from the *absence* of evidence. The model of endorsement distinguishes three rule condition endorsements for inferences of this kind (see section 3.2.5 of this chapter and also Chapter 4). On the other hand, the corroboration endorsement of Figure 3-6 seems to be a different kind of endorsement. It is called a *conclusion endorsement* because it refers to a relationship between two or more conclusions (those of rules 2 and 3 in Fig. 3-1) that are used as evidence. (Besides rule and conclusion endorsements, three other kinds of endorsements are discussed in Chapter 4.)

It is important to distinguish different kinds of endorsements because an intelligent system will respond differently to the different kinds of uncertainty they represent. For example, a natural counter to an overly general rule condition is to find corroborating evidence. The *too general* endorsement warns that the rule´s conclusion may be false even if the condition is true, but it is much less likely that the conclusion is false given corroborating evidence. Similarly, if two conclusions are endorsed as *conflicting*, a natural counter is to try to damage the credibility of the premises of one of the conclusions. This discussion, and particularly the reference to "natural counters" to kinds of uncertainty suggests that endorsements can be used to resolve or discount uncertainty. This is one of the advantages of the model of endorsement. Numeric methods do not have this advantage because degrees of belief summarize information about uncertainty that is required for generating resolutions of uncertainty.

In summary of the discussion of representational adequacy, it seems that the probability theory approach has a great advantage in making *degree* of belief explicit. In the endorsement-based approach it is easy to align evidence pro and con a hypothesis, and it is easy to distinguish different kinds of evidence, but it *can* be relatively difficult to express *how much* one believes something. The model of endorsement does not forbid numerical degrees of belief, but, as we discussed in section 2.3.2, the SOLOMON program is in part an experiment to see how far one can get *without* such numbers. Probability theory also has the advantage of accepting a degree of belief without justification, while in the endorsement-based approach we are interested *only* in the justifications -- the reasons for believing and disbelieving. If, however, the justifications or components of a degree of belief *should* be distinguished, then the "advantage" of the aggregate probability as a representation becomes a liability.

The second dimension on which we were to compare the approaches is the ease of constructing a design -- an arrangement of evidence. Here we see a clear advantage of the endorsement-based approach. The advantage becomes most apparent if we consider the task of writing an AI program to construct Bayesian designs for problems like the Walker-Leakey analysis. It takes a great deal of knowledge and skill to decide upon a partitioning design, to decide which -- if any -- piece of evidence to use to construct prior probabilities and the rest to assess conditionals, and to decide to use likelihood ratios instead of absolute probabilities. Shafer and Tversky's design is very elegant and satisfies their criteria of being "cogent, insightful, thorough, and reliable in its treatment of the evidence."[5] But, as Shafer and Tversky themselves note, the success of using probability theories for analyses of evidence "will often depend on the skill of the user." (p 5.) The pragmatic question I pose here is whether the very simple ledger book approach to

[5] For the purpose of this discussion, we may forgive it the classic Bayesian problem of not knowing how to assign probability in the absence of evidence about hypotheses exclusive of a hypothesis for which there is evidence.

weighing evidence is deficient in comparison with the more complicated designs of probability theory.

A good Bayesian design, according to Shafer and Tversky, is one that does not make unrealistic demands of the person who assesses probabilities for the design. For example, Shafer and Tversky constructed their design to avoid the need for unconditional prior probabilities; instead, the design asks about the *ratios* or likelihoods. It seems, however, that the skill required to construct good Bayesian designs may in fact be a facility to work within the fetters of probability theory. We might characterize the process as follows:

> "We want to know which of several hypotheses is most believable, so let us first make a correspondence between believability and probability, and then ask about the probability of each hypothesis given the available evidence. As a first approximation, let us decide to use the calculus of conditional probability and Bayes´s theorem. However, we find that this requires us to assess a variety of quantities for which there is no corresponding belief, so we must use our mathematical skill to reformulate the original Bayesian design."

It seems that the need for sophisticated Bayesian designs results from trying to recast evidence in terms of probabilities; one often finds that an initial design requires evidence that cannot be confidently assessed. For example, the unconditional probability of a degree of morphological diversity was thought, by Shafer and Tversky, to be too difficult to assess. Instead, they proposed assessing likelihood ratios. A major advantage of the ledger book scheme is that it allows one to align pro and con a hypothesis the evidence one *does* have, without placing demands for evidence that one does *not* have.

It might be argued that the skill required to construct a Bayesian design is not much of an impediment because, for many AI applications, the design needs to be worked out once only. It is certainly the case that MYCIN, for example, did not have and probably did not need the skill to construct a variety of combining functions. On the other hand, it is true that Shortliffe and his colleagues were continually struggling with problems with the CF approach, and that they laid these difficulties at the door of probability theory: "Despite the shortcomings of the CF model, it must be recognized that the issues we were addressing reflect a somewhat groping effort to cope with the limitations of probability theory." (Buchanan and Shortliffe, 1984, Chapter 10.) The initial decision, to combine evidence as if it were statements of probability, led to a variety of problems. The advantage of this approach, however, is that once one agrees to recast evidence as statements of probability, there is a simple calculus for combining evidence. Conversely, although the endorsement-based approach allows one to align arguments in a simple ledger-book design, and although it does not demand evidence that cannot be assessed with confidence, it does require qualitative rules for weighing evidence based on the endorsements of the evidence.

The next section extends the analysis of the Walker-Leakey evidence from the simple case of weighing evidence to the more germane case of using evidence in chains of inferences.

3.4 Multiple Dependent Inferences

The designs of the previous section are what I call *independent inference* designs. By this I mean that no uncertain inference depends on the outcome of another. In the Shafer-Tversky design, five pieces of evidence were weighed directly -- no other evidence depended on them. In the ledger-book designs the conditions of rules 1, 2, and 3 corresponded to the original pieces of Walker and Leakey's evidence, and the conclusions of the rules were not themselves used as evidence for any other inferences. Thus, the previous designs show us just a single frame in an ongoing argument. For example, having concluded, with some degree of belief, that the three-species hypothesis is most likely to be true, Walker and

Leakey then go on to discuss its implications for the theoretical premise that supported the single species hypothesis. They use the conclusion to argue for a favorite Leakey hypothesis, that of *Homo habilis*. They propose that *A. robustus* populations lacked culture. In short, our analyses of their arguments are actually of an admittedly crucial but isolated chunk.

Not only do the Walker-Leakey arguments extend forward from their acceptance of the three-species hypothesis, but also, this conclusion depends on a series of inferences that are not explicit in either the Shafer-Tversky or endorsement-based analyses. For example, much of the argument rests on the conclusion that the three forms represent contemporary populations. There is really no question about speciation if, for example, one form died out before the other appeared. And yet, Walker and Leakey acknowledge that the principal dating method -- dating local volcanic ash or *tuff* -- is inaccurate in the locale of East Turkana:

> Unfortunately for those interested in measuring the rates if evolutionary change in hominid lineages, the difference between the oldest and youngest proposed KBS-tuff dates is some 1.3 million years. ... The KBS-tuff discrepancy is enough to allow uncomfortably different evolutionary rates for various hypothetical hominid lineages.

Another issue is that of morphological variability. It is argued that the *gracile* and *robustus* forms are not of the same species because their dentition is somewhat different, and that the *erectus* form has a large brain case and small teeth, while the other forms have reverse traits. Walker and Leakey argue that the two hypotheses that classify the *gracile* form as female must be rejected because they involve too much sexual dimorphism. But if "too much sexual dimorphism" is evidence, we must ask on what evidence *it* is based. It is not certain by any means that there is too much sexual dimorphism between the *gracile* and *robustus* forms:

> A great deal of variation is often found between the two sexes of a single species. ... Although the variability in the dimensions and proportions of the teeth cannot be matched in living dimorphic populations, there is some hint tht dental dimorphism might have been greater in extinct hominoids. Louis de Bonis of the University of Paris has collected a series of Miocene hominoid jawbones in Macedonia. His sample is from a small area; if the mandibles all belong to the same species, they represent a degree of dimorphism greater than that found in living anthropoid apes. (Walker and Leakey, 1978, p. 66)

Finally, there is the issue of whether *robustus* and *gracile* forms *might* be found in China and Java. Recall that Walker and Leakey use the fact that they had not been found as evidence that they did not exist. Assuming that an effort was made to discover the forms, Walker and Leakey are no doubt justified in their conclusion. In general, however, this kind of inference requires additional support before it is believable.

Thus, the inferences in the analyses in the previous section were based on evidence that was not itself certain. For the sake of simplicity Shafer and Tversky took the evidence as accurate, as I did in the parallel endorsement-based analysis. But it is uncharacteristic of arguments with evidence, especially in diagnostic AI programs, to limit one´s analysis to a single set of independent inferences. In general, uncertain inferences take as premises the conclusions of other uncertain inferences. In such cases, a method is needed to ensure that some characterization of the uncertainty of a premise is represented in its conclusion. This section will show how the endorsement-based approach can be extended to multiple, dependent inferences. It assumes a familiarity with backward chaining control structures, which are discussed in section 2.3.3.2.

A single chain of inferences will be discussed, since that suffices to illustrate the similarities and differences between probabilistic and endorsement-based approaches (other examples of the latter can be found in chapter 4). As in the previous section, Walker and Leakey's arguments will first be converted into inference rules. These will then be assigned endorsements and degrees of belief, and the credibility of successive inferences will be computed.

We will use the previous quote from Walker and Leakey as an example. They are arguing the evidence pro and con hypothesis 2, which is that *A. robustus* and the *gracile* form are male and female of the same species, respectively. *A. robustus* has larger teeth than the *gracile* form. In fact, if the difference in size is due to sexual dimorphism, then it exceeds the degree of dimorphism in any extant dimorphic populations. The question that Walker and Leakey seem to be asking is "To what mechanism should we attribute the differences in dentition: Speciation or dimorphism?" And their answer seems to be "If the mechanism is not dimorphism, then it is speciation." The evidence *for* attributing the difference in dentition to dimorphism is Louis de Bonis' collection of mandibles, while the evidence *against* this attribution is that no living dimorphic populations are so extremely dimorphic.[6]

Table 3-4 shows these arguments represented as inference rules, with degrees of belief and endorsements associated with the inferences. Rule 1 says that if the difference in the size of the teeth (Δ-tooth-size) is not due to dimorphism, then it is due to speciation. This gets a strong degree of belief, marred only by the fact that speciation and dimorphism are not exhaustive alternatives: There is also the possibility of different adaptations within a species, although this is regarded as unlikely. The conclusion is endorsed as **unwarranted** (see section 4.4.3), which means that the rule may have considerable heuristic power but that its condition

[6] Walker and Leakey are indeed saying that if a sexual dimorphism is more extreme than any encountered to date, then it is not a dimorphism at all, but rather, a case of speciation. The dangers of this kind of reasoning are obvious: No logical basis exists to increase the upper bound on degree of dimorphism. There is also a circularity in their argument: If morphological differences are within the bounds of dimorphism, and the fossils are not of different species, then the morphological differences are due to dimorphism (the de Bonis argument). But the only specified method for proving the fossils to be of the same species is to prove dimorphism. I assume that there must be other methods to prove speciation, although they are not discussed by Walker and Leakey.

does not *necessarily* imply the conclusion. The condition is endorsed as a **hard-not**, which means that it is believable only if the expression **(not (due-to dimorphism Δ-tooth-size))** appears in the database. This says, essentially, "You must prove that Δ-tooth-size is not due to dimorphism; it does not suffice to *fail* to prove that Δ-tooth-size is due to dimorphism" (see section 4.4.1.1). Thus, it is a strong endorsement.

The second rule in Table 3-4 provides evidence for Rule 1 that Δ-tooth-size is not due to dimorphism. The rule says, "if Δ-tooth-size exceeds any degree of dimorphism known in extant dimorphic populations, *and* we can assume that there is no historical level of dimorphism greater than that found in extant populations, then we can conclude that Δ-tooth-size is not due to dimorphism."[7] This is a weak argument, because it hinges on the assumption that current degrees of dimorphism equal or exceed any previous degrees of dimorphism. Thus, it gets a low numerical measure of belief. The endorsement, **cwa-not**, indicates a different kind of **not**-clause than that of Rule 1. We cannot prove that there never was greater dimorphism that what we find today, because we can never claim that all fossils have been unearthed. We can only fail to prove that any dimorphism exceeds current dimorphism. The **cwa-not** endorsement says "If you have tried to prove the clause and failed, then the negation of the clause is believable." It is a weaker endorsement than the **hard-not** (see section 4.4.1.1).

[7] Once again, we have difficulty encoding Walker and Leakey's arguments because of a logical inconsistency in their reasoning: If Δ-tooth-size *is* due to dimorphism, then the second premise of rule 2 must be false. This is no mere quibble, but a condemnation of reasoning of the form "if **x** has never happened before, and if y=>(**x** or **z**), then we will believe **z**."

Rule 1:
(If (not (due-to dimorphism Δ-tooth-size))
 Then (due-to speciation Δ-tooth-size))

Degree of belief: 0.8
Endorsements: hard-not
unwarranted

Rule 2:
(If (and (exceed Δ-tooth-size extant-dimorphism)
 (not (exceed historical-dimorphism extant-dimorphism)))
 Then (not (due-to dimorphism Δ-tooth-size)))

Degree of belief: 0.4
Endorsments: cwa-not (clause 2)

Rule 3:
(If (same-species de-Bonis-mandibles)
 Then (exceed historical-dimorphism extant-dimorphism))

Degree of belief: 1.0
Endorsements: exact

Datum 1:
(same-species de-Bonis-mandibles)

Degree of belief: .4
Endorsements: Data-accuracy = low

Datum 2:
(exceed Δ-tooth-size extant-dimorphism)

Degree of belief: 1.0
Endorsments: Data-accuracy = high

Table 3-4: Inferences for reasoning about the dimorphism of *A. robustus* and the *gracile* form.

Rule 3 says that if the de Bonis mandibles are of the same species then there is evidence of historical dimorphism in excess of that of extant species. There is no uncertainty associated with this inference. Datum 1 indicates that there is doubt that the de Bonis mandibles are of the same species, while datum 2 notes that the teeth of *A. robustus* and the *gracile* form definitely exceed the bounds of dimorphism of extant populations.

3.4.1 An Analysis Based on Numerical Degrees of Belief

We now show how a degree of belief is derived for the conclusion of Rule 1. The discussion is simplified by the following assignments:

P_1 = (not (due-to dimorphism Δ-tooth-size))
C_1 = (due-to speciation Δ-tooth-size)

$P_{2,1}$ = (exceed Δ-tooth-size extant-dimorphism)
$P_{2,2}$ = (not (exceed historical-dimorphism extant-dimorphism))
C_2 = (not (due-to dimorphism Δ-tooth-size))

P_3 = (same-species de-Bonis-mandibles)
C_3 = (exceed historical-dimorphism extant-dimorphism)

D_1 = (same-species de-Bonis-mandibles)
D_2 = (exceed Δ-tooth-size extant-dimorphism)

Note that to conclude C_1 we must conclude P_1, which in turn depends on C_2. This latter conclusion cannot be asserted unless (& $P_{2,1}$ $P_{2,2}$) is true. $P_{2,1}$ depends on D_2. $P_{2,2}$ depends on showing the C_3 is *false*. C_3 is inferred from the premise P_3, which corresponds to D_1.

The question we pose in this section is how degrees of belief in the premises are to affect the degrees of belief in the conclusions of inference rules. The Bayesian reasoning outlined in section 2.2.4 does not apply to this problem, because it is used to calculate the weight of several pieces of evidence pro and con a *single* proposition (although Bayesian formulations have been developed to handle uncertainty in evidence).[8] We want a method to make the degree of belief in a conclusion sensitive to the credibility of the conclusion's premises. An intuitive and simple method is simply to multiply the two; for example, if inference P=>Q has a degree of belief of .8 (i.e., *dob*(Q | P) = .8), and inference M=>P is believed with strength .5 (i.e., *dob*(P | M) = .5), then M=>P=>Q with strength of belief .5 × .8 = .4. This approach was illustrated in Figure 2-1. Adams (1976) discusses the assumptions underlying this method.

A further preliminary is necessary before continuing with this example. We noted that $P_{2,2}$ depends on showing (not (exceed historical-dimorphism extant-dimorphism)), but there is no rule in Table 3-4 that makes this conclusion. In theory, a backward-chaining problem solver such as the SOLOMON program should not be able to conclude $P_{2,2}$, but, in fact, SOLOMON is able to base conclusions on the absence of evidence and on negative evidence. In order to see the parallels between the endorsement-based approach to this example and numerical approaches, we must make an assumption:

Note that $P_{2,2}$ = (not C_3). If C_3 was completely false, then its falsehood would provide support for $P_{2,2}$. But, in fact, C_3 is not completely false. It derives some support from D_1, which is identical to its premise. Since C_3 is not completely false (which would support $P_{2,2}$), we need a method to calculate the degree of belief in (not C_3), denoted *dob*(**not** C_3), given a degree of belief in C_3. The following relationship is assumed:

$$dob(\textbf{not } C_3) = 1 - dob(C_3)$$

This relationship is implicit in Bayesian reasoning (see 2.2.4), but is rejected by some researchers and is accordingly one of the arguments for preferring the theory

[8] A glance at the rules in Table 3-4 shows that the premise of each rule is supported by only one piece of evidence. Walker and Leakey are quite stingy with their evidence. The following analysis would be more interesting with multiple pieces of evidence for each premise, but I lack the anthropological expertise to make them up.

of belief functions to the Bayesian approach. The relationship allows one to base support for a conclusion on a *lack* of evidence, whereas the theory of belief functions keeps the effects of negative evidence and a lack of evidence separate. To use the relationship with confidence, one must be assured that lack of evidence for a hypothesis is really the same thing as negative evidence, that the inability to conclude something is equivalent to concluding that it is false. This assurance is given by the *closed-world assumption* (see sections 2.2.1 and 4.4.1.1), which states that if a proposition is true, it can be proved true. Thus, lack of evidence for a proposition implies its falsehood. The closed-world assumption is made for the following example.

We know that the degree of belief in C_1 is .8 if P_1 is entirely trustworthy. This is abbreviated $dob(C_1 \mid P_1) = .8$. But P_1 depends on C_2, the conclusion of rule 2, which is always suspect to some extent (i.e., $dob(C_2 \mid (P_{2,1} \ \& \ P_{2,2})) = .4$. If $P_{2,1}$ and $P_{2,2}$ were definite, then by the multiplicative rule above, $C_1 = .4 \times .8 = .32$. Of course, if some uncertainty in $P_{2,1}$ and $P_{2,2}$ makes the degree of belief in C_2 smaller than .4, then C_1 will be correspondingly smaller. In fact, $P_{2,1}$ is certain: The dimorphism implied by *A. robustus* and the *gracile* form *definitely* exceeds the dimorphism of any extant populations (D2). $P_{2,2}$ is not definite, but it has some support from C_3. As we discussed above, $P_{2,2}$ = (not C_3), so $dob(P_{2,2}) = 1 \ dob(C_3)$. Since rule 3 is a certain inference,

$$dob(C_3) = dob(P_3) = dob(D_1) = .4,$$

and so

$$dob(P_{2,2}) = 1 - .4 = .6.$$

The degrees of belief in the individual premises of rule 2 are $dob(P_{2,1}) = 1.0$ and $dob(P_{2,2}) = .6$. What, then, is the degree of belief for the conjunctive premise $(P_{2,1} \ \& \ P_{2,2})$? A conservative approach (adopted from MYCIN) is to take the minimum degree of belief of all the clauses in a conjunctive as the degree of belief for the entire conjunctive (see Shortliffe and Buchanan, 1975). Given this, $dob(P_{2,1}$ & $P_{2,2})$ is calculated to be min[1.0 , .6] = .6. Then, by the same logic as above, $dob(C_2)$ = .4 × .6 = .24, and

$$dob(C_1) = .8 \times .24 = .192.$$

To summarize, the uncertainty of every premise in rules 1, 2, and 3, must be faithfully represented in the rules' conclusions. This is accomplished by the multiplicative combining function discussed above. Briefly, the conclusion that speciation is responsible for the difference in dentition between *A. robustus* and the *gracile* form depends on P_1, the premise that the difference is not due to dimorphism. Rule 2 is at best a weak argument for the claim that differences in dentition are not due to dimorphism, and, in fact, the available evidence, C_3, provides only suggestive support for the premise of rule 2. Thus, C_2 accrues little support, and in turn provides even less support for C_1. Note that since $P_{2,2}$ = (not C_3), the low degree of belief in C_3 is interpreted as support for $P_{2,2}$. But one must remember that this interpretation depends on the closed-world assumption, mentioned above.

3.4.2 An Endorsement-based Analysis

An endorsement-based analysis, like the probabilistic one, is fairly straightforward. The simplest approach would be to prove C_1 by backward chaining on rules 2 and 3, and to propagate the endorsements associated with each conclusion over to the conclusion it supports. Thus, the endorsements of D_1 and D_2 are propagated to C_3 and C_2, respectively, and the endorsements of C_2 are associated with C_1. Thus, C_1 would carry a complete list of all the reasons for believing and disbelieving all the conclusions upon which it is based. However, there is a complication: A strict backward chaining problem solver will fail to prove the conclusion of rule 2, C_2, because no proposition can be found to match

$P_{2,2}$. Rule 3 concludes that there *is* evidence that historical dimorphism exceeds current dimorphism, while $P_{2,2}$ demands the negation of this conclusion.

The SOLOMON implementation of the model of endorsement, described in the following chapter, attempts to prove C_1 by searching for all rules that conclude P_1. It finds rule 2, and proposes the task of proving the precondition ($P_{2,1}$ & $P_{2,2}$). Note that the second premise of rule 2 is endorsed as a **cwa-not**. This means that the closed-world assumption, discussed in the previous section, holds for any attempt to achieve this premise. SOLOMON then tries to prove (P_1 & P_2) It accepts D_2 as evidence for $P_{2,1}$, judging that **high data-accuracy** is a sufficient endorsement for a piece of data. Then, SOLOMON tries to prove $P_{2,2}$.

The **cwa-not** endorsement of $P_{2,2}$ instructs the program that it must *attempt and fail* to prove **(exceed historical-dimorphism extant-dimorphism)** before it can conclude **(not (exceed historical-dimorphism extant-dimorphism))**. Thus, SOLOMON searches for a rule that concludes **(exceed historical-dimorphism extant-dimorphism)**, which is, of course, rule 3. Having found this rule, SOLOMON constructs the task of proving its premise, P_3. Interestingly, its *motive* for this task is to fail, since failure to prove P_3 will allow it to conclude the superordinate goal C_2. In fact, P_3 is matched with D_1, but this proposition is endorsed as having **low data-accuracy**. Let us assume that this endorsement is inadequate.[9] Then, C_3 is asserted with its negative endorsement of **low data-accuracy**, and C_2, which depends on failing to prove **(exceed historical-dimorphism extant-dimorphism)**, is asserted with its endorsements. Finally, C_1 is asserted. It accrues the endorsements of its preconditions (see section 4.4.6), as well as those associated with rule 1. These assertions and their endorsements are shown in Figure 3-7.

Parenthetically, if the endorsement of D_1 was considered adequate, the

---

[9] The adequacy of endorsements depends on what their propositions are wanted for, so there is no way to say that low data-accuracy is always an inadequate endorsement.

analysis would continue along slightly different lines: C_3 would be asserted and $P_{2,2}$ would therefore fail. C_1 would not be asserted. In the model of endorsement, it is relatively unimportant whether a proposition is asserted, since it is the endorsements of a proposition and not its mere presence in the database that convince one of its credibility. It makes little difference whether our mistrust of C_1 is derived from reading off the endorsements in Figure 3-7, or from tracing the endorsements of the failed attempt to prove C_1.

3.5 A Comparison of the Approaches for Multiple Inference Tasks

All of the comments made about representational adequacy in section 3.3 hold here, too, although an issue that was latent in that section is much more salient here: Walker and Leakey´s reasoning relies on a number of dubious assumptions, of which they seem to be unaware. These are mentioned briefly in the footnotes to the previous section. One great advantage of encoding one´s reasoning into inference rules is that the underlying assumptions must be made explicit, otherwise the desired inferences fail. Moreover, logical inconsistencies become evident immediately. This advantage is not a unique feature of the model of endorsement, of course, but accrues to all approaches that use a formal representation language.

Extending the endorsement approach to multiple inferences does not lessen its chief representational *in*adequacy: It is still difficult to represent the *extent* of a phenomenon or *strength* of belief; for example, we resort to the clumsy expedient of labelling data with "high accuracy" or "low accuracy."[10]

---

[10] Of course, this expedient is required primarily because we do not provide other reasons for believing or disbelieving the data.

$\underline{C_1}$:
(due-to speciation Δ-tooth-size))
From: $(task_{rule-1})$
Children: $(task_{rule-1}\ task_{rule-2})$
Motive: (due-to speciation Δ-tooth-size)
Endorsements:
hard-not (from $task_{rule-1}$)
unwarranted (from $task_{rule-1}$)
cwa-not (from clause 2, $task_{rule-2}$)
data-accuracy = high (from Datum 2)
data-accuracy = low (from Datum 1)

$\underline{C_2}$:
(not (due-to dimorphism Δ-tooth-size))
From: $task_{rule-2}$
Children $(task_{rule-3})$
Motive: (not (due-to dimorphism Δ-tooth-size))
Endorsements:
cwa-not (from clause 2, $task_{rule-2}$)
data-accuracy = high (from Datum 2)
data-accuracy = low (from Datum 1)

$\underline{C_3}$:
(exceed historical-dimorphism extant-dimorphism)
From: $(task_{rule-3})$
Children $(task_{data-1})$
Motive: (not (exceed historical-dimorphism extant-dimorphism))
Endorsements: data-accuracy = low (from Datum 1)

Datum 1:
(same-species de-Bonis-mandibles)
Endorsements: Data-accuracy = low

Datum 2:
(exceed Δ-tooth-size extant-dimorphism)
Endorsments: Data-accuracy = high

Figure 3.7: Endorsements for the conclusions derived during the analysis of section 3.4.2.

As in the previous analysis, we find the numerical approach much more natural for expressing degrees of belief, but, as before, I would caution that we thus relinquish any information that we may later use to justify a belief. Consider the body of endorsements for C_1 in Figure 3-7 ($\mathbf{e_{c1}}$). From these endorsements and the tasks that produced them we can reconstruct the following story:

> We want to prove that the differences in dentition between *A. robustus* and the *gracile* form, Δ-tooth-size, are due to speciation. This required proving first that Δ-tooth-size is not due to dimorphism. It is not sufficient to *fail* to prove that Δ-tooth-size is due to dimorphism; we must prove that it is *not* due to dimorphism. This can be accomplished by rule 2. The first clause of rule 2 is highly credible. The second clause involves proving that no historical dimorphism exceeds the maximum dimorphism of extant species. This cannot be proved but we can fail to disprove it. Thus, we generate from rule 3 the task of proving **(exceed historical-dimorphism extant-dimorphism)** with the *motive* of failing and thus proving **(not (exceed historical-dimorphism extant-dimorphism))**. In fact, this task fails because its premise lacks adequate support, so we can conclude the motive, and, thus, assert the conclusion **(due-to speciation Δ-tooth-size)**. Note, however, that this conclusion is endorsed as **unwarranted**. Note also that while $\text{task}_{\text{rule-1}}$ did not accept simple failure to prove **(due-to dimorphism Δ-tooth-size)**, $\text{task}_{\text{rule-2}}$, which concluded the negation of this clause, did so on the basis of the failure to prove its condition.

This reconstruction used little information that is not explicit in the endorsements dicussed in the previous sections. I think it is fair to say that no numerical approach to reasoning about uncertainty is able to provide this extent of justification for its beliefs.

The information structured in endorsements is not intended for post hoc justifications alone; indeed, it is most useful *during* reasoning. The following chapter describes all the functions of endorsements in reasoning about uncertainty. For the purposes of this analysis, we will focus on the issue of whether a proposition is certain enough to warrant action. In the numerical approach, this inevitably involves a numerical threshold. In the endorsement-based approach the threshold is a qualitative one: We ask whether a proposition is adequately endorsed. One immediate difference between the model of endorsement and numerical approaches is that while the latter use a *constant* numerical threshold, the former recognizes that a proposition may be adequately endorsed for one purpose but not another (although numerical thresholds could be adjustable to different contexts). Thus, the same evidence may or may not provide support, depending on context. This flexibility makes it more difficult to decide whether a proposition is believable; for example, is the conclusion of rule 1 adequately endorsed by $\mathbf{e_{c1}}$? The answer is not obvious, because $\mathbf{e_{c1}}$ contains several endorsements and, more to the point, we do not know what the conclusion is to be used for. Let us focus on a particular question: Are the endorsements of C_2 adequate for C_2 to be used to prove P_1? That is, are we sufficiently impressed with the argument that Δ-tooth-size is *not* due to dimorphism to conclude that the difference is due to speciation?

In the numerical approach, we mistrust C_2 because $dob(C_2) = .24$. In the endorsement-based approach we mistrust it because it is endorsed by **cwa-not**: We know that the only support for C_2 is that we were unable to prove the negation of one of its premises. Now, obviously, this is strong support in cases where two hypotheses (e.g., $P_{2,2}$ and its negation) are exhaustive, and possibly our example is just such a case. Ultimately, the question of whether the **cwa-not** endorsement damns C_2 in the context of P_1 should be decided by a physical anthropologist. It may be that such negative proofs are generally acceptable or unacceptable, or it may be that each case must be decided on its individual evidence. Endorsements represent both general and specific reasons to believe and disbelieve C_2 and other propositions, and we assume criteria for deciding whether these endorsements adequately support their associated propositions. The **cwa-not** endorsement may or may not render C_2 incredible in the context of P_1. The important point is that it provides rich information about *why* C_2 is or is not credible, information that is lacking from numerical degrees of belief.

3.6 Conclusion

The main difference between the numerical approaches and the endorsement-based approach, specifically with respect to chains of inferences, it that reasoning in the former approach is entirely automatic and non-reflective, while the latter approach provides much information for reasoning *about* one´s uncertainty. Consequently, reasoning in the endorsement-based approach can be carefully controlled and determined by the quality, kinds, and availability of evidence.

Endorsements provide the information necessary to many aspects of reasoning about uncertainty: Endorsements are used to schedule sure tasks before unsure ones, to screen tasks before executing them, to determine whether a proposition is certain enough for some purpose, and to suggest new tasks when old ones fail to cope with uncertainty. Endorsements allow one to distinguish different *kinds* of uncertainty, and to tailor reasoning to what is known about uncertainty. Each sophistication of the model of endorsement over numerical reasoning has its cost: Reasoning with numbers is essentially reasoning with implicit and hidden information, and once that information is made explicit, new efforts are required to manage it. Doubtless, some kinds of reasoning about uncertainty do not warrant the extra effort. The next chapter describes the new techniques that are required, how they are implemented in a computer program, and what they accomplish.

4 SOLOMON: An AI Program for Reasoning about Uncertainty

4.1 Introduction

The purpose of this chapter is to show how the model of endorsement outlined in the previous chapters is implemented as a computer program. In the first part of the chapter, a simple problem and SOLOMON´s solution is described. Then we will present the "nuts and bolts" of SOLOMON in progressively more detail, starting with a section on knowledge representation, then one on endorsements, and finally, a section on SOLOMON´s control structure.

A Problem with Uncertainty. Imagine yourself to be an investment counselor, interviewing a client named Spencer. One thing you must establish at some point in the interview is Spencer´s need for favorably taxed income. Two sources of income are taxed at less than the full income tax rates: One is capital gains, and the other is taxfree interest from municipal bonds. Let us concentrate on the latter. You ask yourself "What is an appropriate percentage of taxfree bonds for Spencer?"[1] You could ask Spencer this question, but past experience dictates that Spencer probably would not know how to answer it. That is why he has come to you. Your job is to infer what Spencer wants from what you know about him. Let us assume that Spencer is reticent (or, to change domains momentarily, let us assume that information about a client is expensive to obtain.) All you know about your client is

[1] "Percentage" in this context means fraction of the client´s investable assets. If Spencer asks you to invest $100,000, the question is how many thousands of dollars should go to buy taxfree municipal bonds.

1. He is quite old, not so much in years as in health and attitude

2. He requires quite a lot of money relative to the ability of his capital to produce income.

3. He is in a "medium" tax bracket, say, 35%.

The first two pieces of information are pretty certain, but you have some uncertainty about the third. In general, clients are inaccurate about their tax status, and Spencer's is marginal -- at the high end of what you think of as a "medium" tax liability.

Your chief source of uncertainty, however, is that you do not know much about Spencer, and so you must use weak inference rules to decide on an appropriate percentage of municipal bonds. One very general rule is

> **"clients in a *high* tax bracket, with *low* risk tolerance, should be invested in municipal bonds in proportion to their income needs".**

However, you cannot make this inference because Spencer is not in a high tax bracket and, more importantly, you don't know his risk tolerance. The first of these problems, it seems, might be an impediment to a literal-minded computer program, but it should not pose difficulties for you: Although Spencer *says* his tax bracket is 35%, it could easily be higher, and anyway, the condition that tax-bracket be high is not inflexible in your mind.[2] Thus, you feel inclined to treat Spencer's tax bracket as "high" for the purpose of inferring his taxfree bond need, and the only thing that stands in the way of a recommendation is that you do not know Spencer's risk tolerance. If he will accept a lot of risk, then it is best to buy him stocks with capital gains potential; if he will accept only a little risk you should buy him municipal bonds.

[2] Conditions for other considerations *may* be inflexible; for example, there is a legal age requirement for Spencer to tap into his IRA retirement fund.

The easiest way to get an estimate of a client´s risk tolerance is to ask "What is your risk tolerance?" Unfortunately, the answer is rarely accurate. Sometimes, investment counselors use the client´s current mixture of large stocks and treasury bills to provide an estimate of risk tolerance (see, for example, Sharpe, 1981, p. 584-587). If the client does not have any investments, he or she is asked to imagine a comfortable mix of stocks and treasury bills. Other factors that affect a client´s sensitivity to risk are marital status, age, financial responsibility and the ability to meet it, and the economy. An interview with a client guages these and other factors and provides an investment counselor with an informal measure of risk tolerance. The counselor may decide that the client will accept "zero," "some," "medium," "high," or "very high" risk, depending on the factors just discussed, and also on the quality and consistency of the client´s information. For example, imagine an unmarried computer scientist just out of graduate school with no financial responsibility, a huge income, and a stated preference for risky investments. This is a clear and consistent portrait, and strongly suggests high risk tolerance. But if, in addition, this client appears naive and inclined to blame the investment counselor for poor market performance, then the counselor may well downgrade the client´s risk tolerance a notch or two.[3] It is this kind of informal assessment of risk tolerance from weak evidence that concerns us here; assessments of the risk tolerance parameter -- formally defined as the marginal rate of substitution of risk (the variance of return) for return (Sharpe, 1981) -- can be estimated by the ratio of large stocks to bonds as described above.

Imagine that, in your role as an advisor to Spencer, you know two general rules to infer risk tolerance. First, if your client is old, then infer that his risk tolerance is low. Second, if Spencer needs a lot of income relative to the ability of his capital to produce it, then infer that his risk tolerance is low. Given what

---

[3] I am grateful to Mark Lieberman for these and many other observations.

you already know about Spencer, these rules seem to imply that he is intolerant of risk. Unfortunately, the rules themselves are uncertain. The first is an overgeneralization, since there are plenty of old but daring investors. The second makes intuitive sense -- if there is little spare cash in one´s finances then one is unlikely to risk it -- but it is also overgeneral because the only way to maintain a standard of living from a not-quite-adequate capital base is to invest in something riskier. Many investors make up for the diminishing real interest from their capital assets by buying stocks, and so it is not strictly true that a client is risk averse if he needs more money than his assets can produce in interest. (One might imagine spending out of capital to maintain a standard of living without the risk of stocks; in fact, investors seem extremely reluctant to spend capital, regardless of their age, health, and wealth.) Finally, risk tolerance summarizes an investor´s willingness to *trade* risk for expected return, and so it is difficult to know Spencer´s risk tolerance without knowing what he could get by taking more risk. Thus, you are uncertain about Spencer´s risk tolerance because both of the rules that you might use to infer it introduce uncertainty.

However, notice that your two estimates of Spencer´s risk tolerance agree -- both suggest that he is risk averse. Given this corroboration, the effect of the uncertainty of each individual estimate can be minimized. You feel comfortable, if not certain, with the conclusion that Spencer´s risk tolerance is low, just as you are willing to believe that his tax bracket is high. Given this information you conclude that Spencer requires taxfree municipal bonds in his portfolio, in a percentage that is proportional to his income need.

This example illustrates several criteria for a model of reasoning about uncertainty (see also section 2.3.2). Note first that different kinds of knowledge are involved: knowledge about the likelihood of an accurate response, knowledge about the effect of corroboration on certainty, and knowledge about uncertainty introduced by overgeneral inference rules. In the model of endorsement, this knowledge about reasons to believe and disbelieve conclusions is represented in endorsements. Another observation is that there seemed to be no need to express *how much* we believed the conclusions about Spencer's tax-bracket, risk-tolerance, and taxfree bond need.[4] In lieu of assigning degrees of belief to these conclusions, we accepted the conclusions as *certain enough* and noted why they were uncertain. A third criterion is that reasoning about uncertainty requires flexibility. Recall that our first inference required Spencer's tax bracket to be high, when it was actually an uncertain 35%. Given our uncertainty about Spencer's tax bracket, we were satisfied that it *might* be high. Note also that our willingness to accept a result depends on what we want it for. We were willing to accept a corroboration of two pieces of evidence as reason enough to believe Spencer was intolerant of risk, at least for the purpose of recommending a percentage of municipal bonds. However, if our goal had been to decide on relative percentages of blue-chip and high-technology growth stocks (a "finer" distinction), we might have demanded more compelling evidence.

The next section briefly describes SOLOMON, a program that reasons in much the same style as we have discussed. SOLOMON's approach to the problem of Spencer's investments is presented.

4.2 SOLOMON and the Problem of Investments for Spencer

SOLOMON is a backward-chaining problem solver that proves assertions represented in first-order predicate calculus. (See Sections 2.3.3.1 and 2.3.3.2 for introductions to predicate calculus and backward chaining, respectively.) Many of the examples in this chapter are from the domain of portfolio management and an

[4] In fact, I'd go so far as to suggest that assigning numbers to these conclusions would have appeared artificial, as if we were trying to force plausible reasoning into a numerical mold. But Professor Shortliffe has pointed out that in this example, all evidence agrees, and so there is no need to assess the net weight of conflicting evidence. He suggests that in the case of conflict it is natural to use numbers as net weights. But see section 2.3.4.

expert system called FOLIO (Cohen and Lieberman, 1983), but SOLOMON is intended to provide a general framework for reasoning about uncertainty. SOLOMON uses endorsements (see Sections 4.4 and 2.3), to reason about issues of control, to resolve and discount uncertainty, and to decide when propositions are believable enough to use in further reasoning.

The problem of determining Spencer's taxfree bond need is a typical one for SOLOMON. To solve it, SOLOMON first collects all rules that conclude about taxfree bond needs, then it attempts to prove the rules' preconditions. The preconditions themselves become goals, more rules are collected, and the cycle continues until the preconditions of the original goal are satisfied, or until there are no longer any ways to prove the preconditions. This approach to problem solving has a long history in AI (e.g., Green, 1969). However, since SOLOMON must deal with uncertain propositions and their endorsements, it differs in a number of crucial respects from its historical predecessors.

4.2.1 An Example of SOLOMON

The similarities and differences between SOLOMON and straightforward backward chainers are illustrated in the following example. (Sections 2.3.3.1 and 2.3.3.2) provide introductions to the predicate calculus representation and backward-chaining control structure used in this and later examples.) SOLOMON's problem can be stated:

(taxfree-bond-need spencer ?level),

where **?level** is the variable whose value SOLOMON seeks. As initial data, SOLOMON knows these three clauses:

```
datum-00031 ≡ (tax spencer medium)
datum-00025 ≡ (income-need spencer high)
datum-00028 ≡ (age spencer high)
```

and three inference rules:

TFBN-1:

```
(if  (and  (tax ?client high)
           (risk-tolerance ?client low))
 then (taxfree-bond-need ?client
                  (proportional income-need)))
```

RTI-1:

```
(if   (income-need ?client high)
 then (risk-tolerance ?client low))
```

RTI-2:

```
(if   (age ?client high)
 then (risk-tolerance ?client low))
```

To prove **(taxfree-bond-need spencer ?level)**, SOLOMON first generates a task from rule **TFBN-1**, and then decides whether this task is worth running. This step screens out tasks that do not contribute anything to SOLOMON´s certainty in the goal it is trying to prove. SOLOMON determines that the task is adequately endorsed. Currently, any task is adequately endorsed, provided that its conclusion is not redundant with an already-believed conclusion. But, in general, a task may be accepted or rejected depending on the rule endorsements of the rule from which the task was derived:

```
In Task-endorsed-ok. Task = task-00037
Task is to prove =
    (taxfree-bond-need spencer (proportional income-need))
task-00037 is adequately endorsed.
```

The condition of **TFBN-1**, and thus, of **task-00037** is

(and (tax spencer high) (risk-tolerance spencer low)).

SOLOMON checks whether this clause is satisfied by the available data, and finds that **datum-00031** supports **(tax spencer high)**, but that the other clause lacks support.

```
Task-db =(nil)
Enter run-task. Task = task-00037
Condition = (and (tax spencer high)
                 (risk-tolerance spencer low))
Action = (taxfree-bond-need spencer
                 (proportional income-need))
On db? = nil
curr-end  (tax spencer high): (good datum-00031)
curr-end  (risk-tolerance spencer low): nil
```

Note that **datum-00031** is not **(tax spencer high)**, but **(tax spencer medium)**; but, since it was specified in the a priori rule endorsement of rule **TFBN-1** that **(tax ?client high)** is an approximate clause, SOLOMON accepts **datum-00031** as satisfactory. The notation **(good datum-00031)** is not intended to construe that **datum-00031** is *true*, but rather, that it is certain enough for the purpose of achieving **task-00037**.

Since SOLOMON does not know any propositions of the form **(risk-tolerance spencer low)**, it generates subgoals to conclude this goal. They derive from rules **RTI-1** and **RTI-2**, and result in tasks **00038** and **00039**. As before, SOLOMON checks whether these tasks are worth executing, but finds that both are to be rejected. A criticism has been discovered against the domain rules **RTI-1** and **RTI-2**. The former rule states that high income need implies low tolerance for risk to interest, and the latter uses advanced age to imply low risk tolerance. Each are suspect because it may be too general: Not *all* old clients are risk-averse, and not *all* clients who need lots of income are risk-averse. The conditions of these rules admit more people to the class of those averse to risk to interest than are warranted and, thus, in contexts where one wishes to be especially sure of one´s results, they are too general. For the sake of this illustration, rules have been set up to reject tasks endorsed as **maybe-too-general**. (In other contexts, this negative endorsement would not necessarily condemn its associated task.)

In Task-endorsed-ok. Task = task-00038
Task is to prove = (risk-tolerance spencer low)

Task is rejected for being too general

In Task-endorsed-ok. Task = task-00039
Task is to prove = (risk-tolerance spencer low)

Task is rejected for being too general

SOLOMON has run out of ways to prove that Spencer´s risk tolerance is low, or, at least, it has run out of subgoals derived by the classic backward-chaining subgoal mechanism (see section 4.4.1.3). But SOLOMON is often able to propose alternative tasks when it runs out of those derived in a standard fashion. The proposed alternative, which it believes will discount its uncertainty of **task-00038** and **task-00039**, is the *resolution task* **res-00046**, whose condition is the union of the conditions of **task-00038** and **task-00039**. SOLOMON uses the heuristic that if the condition of a task is too general, but another task on the agenda draws the same conclusion, then solving both tasks and achieving corroborating evidence is apt to increase one´s certainty. SOLOMON knows that **task-00038** and **task-00039** conclude the same thing because whenever it puts tasks on the agenda, it endorses them as potentially corroborating or contradicting tasks that are already there (see section 4.4).

```
In Task-endorsed-ok. Task = res-00046
Task is to prove = (risk-tolerance spencer low)
res-00046 is adequately endorsed.

Task-db =(nil)
Enter run-task. Task = res-00046
Condition = (and (income-need spencer high)
                 (age spencer high))
Action = (risk-tolerance spencer low)
On db? = (good datum-00025 datum-00028)
```

Both **datum-00025** and **datum-00028** are adequately endorsed; they are endorsed only as having **(data-accuracy = high)** , which SOLOMON accepts, when it is the sole endorsement, as an adequate endorsement in all contexts.

```
Endorsement data-end-00026.
    (data-type ((= . interview))
     data-accuracy ((= . high)))
Endorsement data-end-00029.
    (data-type ((= . interview))
       data-accuracy ((= . high)))
```

SOLOMON now asserts the conclusion of **res-00046, (risk-tolerance spencer low)**, and returns to the parent task of **res-00046** to attempt, once again, to prove its condition. But before attempting **task-00037** it checks whether the task is still worth running -- that nothing has happened since the last attempt to disqualify the task:

```
Asserting (risk-tolerance spencer low)

In Task-endorsed-ok. Task = task-00037
Task is to prove = (taxfree-bond-need spencer
                        (proportional income-need))
task-00037 is adequately endorsed.

Task-db =(nil)
Enter run-task. Task = task-00037
Condition = (and (tax spencer high)
                 (risk-tolerance spencer low))
Action = (taxfree-bond-need spencer
                 (proportional income-need))
On db? = (good datum-00031 conc-00050)
```

SOLOMON finds **datum-00031** in support of **(tax spencer high)** and **conc-00050** supporting **(risk-tolerance spencer low)**. The reasons for believing these conclusions are shown below. First, **datum-00031**, is endorsed as being derived from the interview and having medium data-accuracy. Conclusion **conc-00050**, has three endorsements. First, it is derived from a resolution of uncertainty based on a corroboration of the conclusions of **task-00038** and **task-00039**. Additionally, the data that support the condition of **res-00046** are endorsed as having high data-accuracy:

```
The endorsements of the preconditions
(datum-00031 conc-00050):

Endorsement data-end-00032.
            (data-type ((= . interview))
             data-accuracy ((= . medium)))

Endorsment conc-end-00051.
        Prop               : (risk-tolerance spencer low)
        Preconditions   : (datum-00025 datum-00028)
        Concluding task : res-00046
        From domain rule: nil
Endorsement res-end-00047.   From frame : res-00046
```

```
                resolution  ((= . p-corroborate-res))
                components  ((= task-00038 task-00039)))
        Endorsement data-end-00026.   From frame : datum-00025
                (data-type ((= . interview))
                 data-accuracy ((= . high)))
        Endorsement data-end-00029.   From frame : datum-00028
                (data-type ((= . interview))
                 data-accuracy ((= . high)))
```

Finally, SOLOMON asserts its original goal:

Asserting (taxfree-bond-need spencer (proportional income-need)).

In summary, SOLOMON tries to prove a task with a conjunctive condition (**task-00037**) and finds that the first but not the second clause is satisfied. The data that matches the first clause is believable -- not "true," but believable enough for the purposes of proving the first clause of **task-00037**. The second clause, **(risk-tolerance spencer low)**, results in two tasks, **00038** and **00039** that SOLOMON rejects on the grounds that their conditions are too general. SOLOMON has now exhausted the conventionally-derived subgoals of **(risk-tolerance spencer low)**. Conventional backward chaining systems would have to quit work, with their uncertainty about **(taxfree-bond-need spencer ?level)** unresolved. SOLOMON, on the other hand, recognizes kinds of uncertainty and knows about appropriate resolutions; in particular, it knows that potentially corroborating tasks that are rejected for having too-general conditions can be merged into a single task with a conjunctive condition. Should this condition be met, the conclusion is supported by corroborating evidence. This is, in fact, what happened, and SOLOMON was able to prove **res-00046** and return to prove **task-00037**.

The representation and kinds of knowledge that SOLOMON required to solve this problem are discussed in the next section.

4.3 Representation of Knowledge in SOLOMON

Reasoning in SOLOMON is facilitated by several kinds of declarative and procedural knowledge. Some knowledge is used primarily for record-keeping; for example, the **p-corroboration** endorsement is an endorsement that notes a potential corroboration between tasks on the agenda. It is a message saying "I have noticed a potential corroboration." Constructing this endorsement has no side-effects, although other processes can use the information to their own ends. On the other hand, SOLOMON has some procedural knowledge that tells it how to build resolution tasks such as **res-00046** in section 4.2. The more passive knowledge is discussed first, and the more active knowledge in the subsection after that.

4.3.1 Data Structures: Introduction

SOLOMON uses ten kinds of objects to reason about a problem. These are domain rules, data, conclusions, tasks, and resolutions, and each is associated with a characteristic kind of endorsement. Domain rules are encodings of human expert knowledge; in the current implementation of SOLOMON they are portfolio management heuristics from the expert system FOLIO. Data are pieces of knowledge that are supplied by the user during a consultation; conclusions are the results of domain inferences. Tasks are instantiations of domain rules and are put onto an agenda to await action. Resolutions are tasks that are generated by SOLOMON when none of the tasks on its agenda contribute sufficiently to its certainty.

All these objects are represented as frames; for example, domain rules are frames with a *condition* slot and an *action* slot, and an indefinite number of *rule-endorsements* -- which are themselves nested frames.[5] I have found this structure useful for several reasons. First, when thinking about what makes a piece of knowledge uncertain it helps to know which characteristics of the knowledge are important. For example, salient characteristics of a piece of evidence are those that are questioned in legal proceedings (e.g., Loftus, 1979): the reliability of its source, how the source produces the evidence, and the conditions under which the evidence was evoked or obtained. It matters little whether the source produces evidence with a Southern accent, and it rarely matters whether the evidence is a written document or spoken testimony. These are less important characteristics, and one´s certainty is less likely to be perturbed as these characteristics are altered.

A second reason for the frame representation of knowledge in SOLOMON is that it is a hierarchical scheme that facilitates property inheritance and using defaults (Minsky, 1975; Barr and Feigenbaum, 1981, Chapter 3). For example, one general method for producing resolution tasks when there is an unresolvable conflict of conclusions is to "split the difference" -- to create a task that concludes something minimally different from the conflicting conclusions. In the absence of other information, conflicting evidence about the risk tolerance of a widow might be resolved this way. On the other hand, we might have some methods for resolving questions about risk tolerance that are specific to widows, such as "accept the lowest estimate." Thus, the hierarchical structure of knowledge in SOLOMON permits one to specify both very general and very specific methods for reasoning about uncertainty.

Some of the slots in SOLOMON´s frames contain procedures. For example, frames for the endorsements of *if* clauses in domain rules specify how to determine whether a clause is believable. Thus, a third advantage of the frame representation in SOLOMON is that it allows one to mix procedural and

[5] The prototype functions for SOLOMON´s representation were taken from Charniak, Riesbeck, and McDermott, (1980).

declarative knowledge. And, as I discussed above, if SOLOMON is to have a metalanguage to specify the effects of endorsements on its behavior, the vocabulary of the language will be made up of the kinds of procedures mentioned here.

The following section illustrates the knowledge structures used by SOLOMON for the example at the beginning of this chapter (section 4.2). These are presented in an exhaustive format for the sake of completeness, and some are redundant. The structure of endorsements is touched on briefly, but is discussed in detail in section 4.4. The casual reader should note that endorsements are associated with rules, tasks, conclusions, data, and resolutions; and, note the inheritance of default slot values. This done, the casual reader may skip to section 4.3.3.

4.3.2 Knowledge Structures Generated During the Example

The frame structures discussed here have nested structures. Each frame has a *name*, and an indefinite number of *slots*. Each slot has an indefinite number of *aspect-value* pairs. A very simple frame is:

NAME:	**Elephant**		
	SLOT:	**Type**	
		ASPECT:	**=**
		VALUE :	**Mammal**
	SLOT:	**Size**	
		ASPECT:	**=**
		VALUE:	**Very-big**
	SLOT:	**Diet**	
		ASPECT:	**if-needed**
		VALUE:	**Vegetarian**
	SLOT:	**Color**	
		ASPECT:	**if-added**
		VALUE:	**Gray**

This is the "elephant" frame. An elephant is an object of (Type = Mammal). Note that this is a (SLOT ASPECT VALUE) triple. Similarly, an elephant is an object of (Size = Very-big). Another kind of ASPECT is illustrated in the third slot of this frame, which describes an elephant as of (Diet if-needed Vegetarian). The if-needed aspect says, "Unless and until we have a slot that specifies the diet (a slot whose ASPECT is ´=´) , assume the diet is vegetarian." Finally, we note that an elephant has (Color if-added Gray). The if-added slot is used to fill-in characteristics of instances of the Elephant frame, that is, when frames are constructed whose (Type = Elephant). Whenever such a frame is constructed, the if-added slot of the Elephant frame specifies that this new frame should have the slot (Color = Gray).

Frames can be nested within one another. The most typical case of this is where endorsement frames are nested within rules, tasks, conclusions, data, and resolutions. This kind of structure is illustrated in the frame for **TFBN-1**, below.

In the examples that follow, we will not specify the ASPECT of a slot if it is "=".

The first structure we will discuss is the **flexible** rule-endorsement. Any clause that is endorsed as being flexible can inherit, from this rule-endorsement, a default value for its **propmatch-if** slot. This slot specifies the method that SOLOMON is to use to determine whether a proposition on the database matches a given goal (see section 4.4.1.3 for more detail). For the **flexible** rule-endorsement, the method is to compare the two with the **approximate** function. When a clause of a rule is endorsed as being flexible, the if-added slots of this endorsement (and those of its ancestors) are activated.

```
------------------------
NAME: flexible   TYPE: rule-end
    SLOT: clause
        ASPECT: if-added
        VALUE : (or (get-val *form* ´propmatch-if)
                    (addspec-e *form* ´propmatch-if ´=
                              ´(lambda (p c) (approximate p c))))
------------------------
```

For example, the clause **(tax ?client high)** in the frame for rule TFBN-1 (see below), is endorsed as being **flexible**. As a result, the if-added slot of the **flexible** endorsement (above) is activated. The variable ***form*** is set to **rule-end-00006**, which is the name of the **flexible** endorsement nested in the frame for **TFBN-1**. The if-added slot of the **flexible** endorsement, illlustrated above, says, "Either **rule-end-00006** already has a **propmatch-if** slot, or I am going to add to **rule-end-00006** the slot **(´propmatch-if ´= ´(lambda(p c)(approximate p c))**.

Of course, **flexible** is not the most general rule-endorsement known to SOLOMON. A more general form is **rule-end**:

```
------------------------
NAME: rule-end   TYPE: end
    SLOT: clause
        ASPECT: if-added
        VALUE :     (or (get-val *form* ´propmatch-if)
                        (addspec-e *form* ´propmatch-if´=
                                  ´(lambda (p c) (equal p c))))
                    (or (get-val *form* ´rulematch-if)
                        (addspec-e *form* ´rulematch-if ´=
                                  ´(lambda (p c) (unify-act p c)))))
------------------------
```

The if-added slots of this structure, too, are checked when a rule-endorsement is created. For example, in the structure shown immediately below -- the frame for the domain rule **TFBN-1** -- **rule-end-00006** has inherited its

propmatch-if property from the **flexible** endorsement, and its **rulematch-if** slot from the general **rule-end** structure, above. The default value for **propmatch-if** is not inherited from **rule-end**, because a more specific value has already been inherited from **flexible**. The **rulematch-if** property has much in common with the **propmatch-if** property: It specifies a method for finding rules whose conclusions match a current goal; the default method specified in **rule-end** is just to find a rule whose conclusion *unifies*. (See section 2.3.3.2 for an introduction to unification.)

The structure below shows the rule **TFBN-1** with all its clauses endorsed. I have just discussed how the endorsement of the clause **(tax ?client high)** is constructed by inheriting properties from more general rule-endorsements. Its interpretation, in English is roughly "This clause need not be satisfied exactly." When SOLOMON looks for rules whose conclusions will satisfy this clause, it searches the conclusion-slots of rules for propositions that unify with **(tax ?client high)**. But when it checks whether the database contains a proposition that satisfies this clause, it will accept a proposition that approximates **(tax ?client high)**, such as, **(tax fred medium)**.

The endorsement of the second clause in the condition of **TFBN-1** -- **rule-end-00007** -- is of type **exact**. It inherits its **propmatch-if** and **rulematch-if** properties directly from the general **rule-end** frame. Its interpretation differs from that of **rule-end-00006** in that it does not permit approximate matches between its clause and propositions on the database:

NAME: TFBN-1 TYPE: domain-rule

SLOT: condition

VALUE : (and (tax ?client high) (risk-tolerance ?client low))

SLOT: action

VALUE : (taxfree-bond-need ?client

```
                (proportional  income-need)
SLOT: rule-end-00006
    VALUE :
            ------------------------
            NAME: flexible-00010  TYPE: flexible
                SLOT: parent
                    VALUE : TFBN-1
                SLOT: clause
                    VALUE : (tax ?client high)
                SLOT: propmatch-if
                    VALUE : (lambda (p c) (approximate p c))
                SLOT: rulematch-if
                    VALUE : (lambda (p c) (unify-act p c))
            ------------------------
SLOT: rule-end-00007
    VALUE :
            ------------------------
            NAME: exact-00011   TYPE: exact
                SLOT: parent
                    VALUE : TFBN-1
                SLOT: clause
                    VALUE : (risk-tolerance ?client low)
                SLOT: propmatch-if
                    VALUE : (lambda (p c) (equal p c))
                SLOT: rulematch-if
                    VALUE : (lambda (p c) (unify-act p c))
            ------------------------
            ------------------------
------------------------
```

Note that **TFBN-1** has a conjunctive condition. In fact, the only logical operators permitted in the conditions of SOLOMON´s tasks are AND and NOT. One is free to specify arbitrarily complex conditions for *rules*, but when tasks are derived from these rules, the initial conditions go through a variety of logical transformations. A rule of the form **(if (or X Y) then (Z))** is transformed into *two* tasks, one of the form **(if (X) then (Z))** and another of the form **(if (Y) then (Z))**.

The frame for **RTI-1**, below, shows that its condition is endorsed as being **maybe-too-general**. That is, the rule-endorsement associated with clause **(income-need ?client high)** is of type **maybe-too-general**. This endorsement does not involve **propmatch-if** and **rulematch-if** properties different from those of the default rule-end frame. The effect of the endorsement is on other aspects of SOLOMON´s processing; for example, the task derived from this rule was rejected in the example given at the beginning of this chapter (section 4.2).

```
---------------------------
NAME: RTI-1   TYPE: domain-rule
    SLOT: condition
          VALUE : (income-need ?client high)
    SLOT: action
          VALUE : (risk-tolerance ?client low)
    SLOT: rule-end-00018
          VALUE :
                  ---------------------------
                  NAME: maybe-too-general-00019   TYPE: maybe-too-general
                        SLOT: parent
                              VALUE : RTI-1
                        SLOT: clause
                              VALUE : (income-need ?client high)
                        SLOT: propmatch-if
                              VALUE : (lambda (p c) (equal p c))
                        SLOT: rulematch-if
                              VALUE : (lambda (p c) (unify-act p c))
                  ---------------------------
---------------------------
```

Rules should be fairly easy to specify in SOLOMON. Rule frames have just condition and action slots, and an indeterminate number of rule-endorsement slots. I have found that creating rule frames by hand is very time-consuming, and a simple rule-editor should be constructed to overcome these problems. In fact, one could build a very sophisticated rule-editor that uses rule-endorsements – records of reasons for believing and disbelieving rules – to help an expert organize his or her knowledge. This proposal is discussed further in Chapter 5.

Currently, one is permitted to specify *one* rule-endorsement per conditional clause; for example, each clause in the condition of **TFBN-1** has just a single endorsement. This is a limitation because, as we shall see in section 4.4, rule-endorsements are not mutually exclusive. However, if more than one rule-endorsement per clause is specified, there is the possibility that two or more **rulematch-if** or **propmatch-if** properties will be applicable, and SOLOMON won´t know which to use. Clearly, this is a temporary problem.

The next structure is that of a datum. Data have just a **prop** slot that state their messages to SOLOMON (e.g., **(tax spencer medium)** and, of course, data-endorsements. The slots of data-endorsements include information about where the data came from (its **data-type**), and information about its accuracy:

```
-----------------------
NAME: datum-00031   TYPE: datum
     SLOT: prop
          VALUE : (tax spencer medium)
     SLOT: data-end-00032
          VALUE :
                    -----------------------
                    NAME: data-end-00033   TYPE: data-end
                         SLOT: data-type
                              VALUE : interview
                         SLOT: data-accuracy
                              VALUE : medium
                    -----------------------
-----------------------
```

In the course of solving the problem at the beginning of this chapter, both tasks **00038** and **00039** were rejected because their condition clauses were considered too-general and, in their place, a *resolution* task was proposed and evaluated. The structure of this task is shown below. It is a resolution of type **p-corroborate-res** – which is the name given to resolutions that attempt to find corroborations between the conclusions of tasks on the agenda. The slots of **res-00046** include information about the original task whose failure prompted the resolution, and about the tasks that are being combined in the resolution. In addition, a resolution has all the typical task slots: A motive, a condition, an action, and the ancestor whose own viability depends on satisfying this resolution. Resolutions also have **resolution-endorsements**, although these currently contribute little information.

```
--------------------------
NAME: res-00046   TYPE: p-corroborate-res
    SLOT: original-task
        VALUE : task-00039
    SLOT: components
        VALUE : (task-00038 task-00039)
    SLOT: res-end-00047
        VALUE :
                    --------------------------
                    NAME: res-end-00048   TYPE: res-end
                        SLOT: resolution
                            VALUE : p-corroborate-res
                        SLOT: components
                            VALUE : (task-00038 task-00039)
                    --------------------------
    SLOT: to-do
        VALUE : prove-condition
    SLOT: motive
        VALUE : (risk-tolerance spencer low)
    SLOT: parent-task
        VALUE : task-00037
    SLOT: condition
        VALUE : (and (income-need spencer high) (age spencer high))
    SLOT: action
        VALUE : (risk-tolerance spencer low)
--------------------------
```

The **motive** slot of tasks bears discussion. It is used primarily to check whether the motive for proposing a task has already been accomplished. For example, if the motive for proposing a task, say, **task-00062**, is to prove **(not (color block red))**, then **task-00062** will not be executed if some other task, say, **task-00057**, has already concluded something with the same motive. However, the "something" that **task-00057** concludes need not be **(not (color block red))**. It may instead be **(color block green)**, but the *motive* for **task-00057** is **(not (color block red))**. Thus, the conclusion of a task need not be identical to its motive, and the motive, not the conclusion, is used to determine whether a goal has already been accomplished.

The last structure I will illustrate, **conc-00050**, is the conclusion posted on SOLOMON´s database when the conditions of **res-00046** were satisfied. It is largely redundant with **res-00046**. In general, conclusions share much of the structure of the tasks that post them, while these in turn share much with the rules from which they are derived.

```
NAME: conc-00050   TYPE: conclusion
    SLOT: prop
        VALUE : (risk-tolerance spencer low)
    SLOT: from-domain-rule
        VALUE : nil
    SLOT: concluding-task
        VALUE : res-00046
    SLOT: preconditions
        VALUE : (datum-00028 datum-00025)
    SLOT: not-preconditions
        VALUE : nil
    SLOT: res-end-00047
        ASPECT: from-frame
        VALUE : res-00046
```

ASPECT: =

VALUE :

NAME: res-end-00048 TYPE: res-end

SLOT: resolution

VALUE : p-corroborate-res

SLOT: components

VALUE : (task-00038 task-00039)

SLOT: data-end-00029

ASPECT: from-frame

VALUE : datum-00028

ASPECT: =

VALUE :

NAME: data-end-00030 TYPE: data-end

SLOT: data-type

VALUE : interview

SLOT: data-accuracy

VALUE : medium

SLOT: data-end-00026

ASPECT: from-frame

VALUE : datum-00025

ASPECT: =

VALUE :

NAME: data-end-00027 TYPE: data-end

SLOT: data-type

VALUE : interview
SLOT: data-accuracy
VALUE : high

Note that conclusions carry endorsements accrued throughout a chain of reasoning. This is because a conclusion adopts all the endorsements of its preconditions, which may themselves be conclusions. This seems a good default rule for propagating endorsements over inferences, since one always has a complete record of the reasons for believing and disbelieving a conclusion. However, it is a very cumbersome policy. I suspect that some interesting psychological principles for *dropping* endorsements from a conclusion may be discovered. This is discussed further in section 4.4.6 and chapter 5.

4.3.3 Procedural Knowledge in SOLOMON

SOLOMON uses endorsements to help it schedule and screen tasks, to decide when a result is certain enough to use, and to propose resolution tasks for intolerably uncertain results. The knowledge it requires for these processes is not associated with endorsements themselves, but rather, is distributed over a number of LISP functions.

4.3.3.1 An Endorsement-ranking Scheme

Scheduling of tasks on the agenda is managed by ranking the *rule-endorsements* of tasks (see section 4.4.1). Since rule-endorsements are an expert´s a priori reasons for believing and disbelieving an inference rule, scheduling tasks by rule-endorsement ensures that SOLOMON uses first those rules that the expert likes best. Currently, the comparison of rule endorsements for ranking purposes is accomplished very simply: Each task may have one inference-type endorsement, several rule-condition endorsements, and one rule-conclusion endorsement. Denote these sets of endorsements **i**, **c**, and **a**. Then, the set of all inference-type endorsements is divided into two subsets $\mathbf{I}^+$ and $\mathbf{I}^-$, as are the sets of rule-condition endorsements and rule-conclusion endorsements. These subsets are roughly "preferred endorsements" and "not so good or downright bad" endorsements, respectively. In this simple scheme, neutral endorsements are not distinguished from reasons to disbelieve; obviously, three subsets of endorsements, $\mathbf{I}^+, \mathbf{I}^0$ and $\mathbf{I}^-$, might have been used instead. The endorsements of two agenda tasks are compared to determine which task is to be executed first: If $\mathbf{i}_1 \cap \mathbf{I}^+ \neq \varnothing$ and $\mathbf{i}_2 \cap \mathbf{I}^+ \neq \varnothing$, then there are "good reasons" for both task_1 and task_2, and rule-condition endorsements are used to break the tie. Similarly, if $\mathbf{c}_1 \cap \mathbf{C}^+ \neq \varnothing$ and $\mathbf{c}_2 \cap \mathbf{C}^+ \neq \varnothing$, then there is still no basis to choose between the tasks, and rule-conclusion endorsements are used to break the tie. Ties that remain after this step are resolved arbitrarily. SOLOMON also regards $\mathbf{i}_1 \cap \mathbf{I}^- \neq \varnothing$ and $\mathbf{i}_2 \cap \mathbf{I}^- \neq \varnothing$ as a tie, although it tests for this condition after checking for membership in the set $\mathbf{I}^+$. Since there are reasons to *disbelieve* both tasks (or at least not strong reasons to believe them), SOLOMON tries to find support for one or both tasks by checking for membership in the set $\mathbf{C}^+$, and so on. SOLOMON ranks one task before another if the first task has a positive endorsement at some level and the other task has a negative endorsement at the same level, for example, if $\mathbf{i}_1 \cap \mathbf{I}^+ \neq \varnothing$ and $\mathbf{i}_2 \cap \mathbf{I}^- \neq \varnothing$.

There are several problems with this ranking scheme. For one, in theory a rule may have both positive and negative rule-condition endorsements, which means that task_1 may have $\mathbf{i}_1 \cap \mathbf{I}^+ \neq \varnothing$ and $\mathbf{i}_1 \cap \mathbf{I}^- \neq \varnothing$. Secondly, the two-group breakdown is not very discriminating between endorsements (although the above scheme is easily generalized to several ranked groups). Despite these and other problems, the scheme works adequately for the small problems that have been run in SOLOMON.

4.3.3.2 Screening Tasks

Tasks are screened in SOLOMON before they are executed. When a task is scheduled, SOLOMON believes there is reason to run it, but between the times it is put on and popped off the agenda, the worth of the task may have diminished. By "worth" I mean something very specific: A task is worth running if it contributes to SOLOMON's certainty in a hypothesis, and it should be abandoned otherwise. The best example of screening knowledge, and the only one that runs in SOLOMON, is, "A task is not worth running if it concludes something that is already adequately endorsed." Other kinds of screening knowledge that are not implemented could be used to determine the "style" of SOLOMON's processing. For example, a "confirmatory" style could be had from the screening rule, "A task is not worth running if it concludes something that may conflict with a previous and adequately-endorsed result." Given this rule SOLOMON would fasten onto a hypothesis and ignore all tasks that conclude anything contrary to it. This is not necessarily a good thing, but one may wish to specify such screening behaviors as part of a psychological -- if not normative -- model.

4.3.3.3 Deciding that an Endorsement is Adequate

The most frequently-used knowledge in SOLOMON determines whether a result is adequately endorsed, whether it is believable enough for some purpose. It includes rules such as "**if the proposition is endorsed by conflict, then it is inadequately endorsed**" and "**if the clause is not a supportive clause and the data for the clause is of low accuracy, then the clause is inadequately endorsed.**" These rules are intended to implement SOLOMON's sensitivity to context. That is, the rules should include conditions that ask about SOLOMON's current goal. The previous rule, for example, says that SOLOMON requires better evidence if its intention is to prove a non-supportive clause than a supportive one. Since SOLOMON uses mostly general endorsements, and has been tested with very simple problems, there has been little opportunity to explore the effects of different contexts on the adequacy of endorsements. The model of endorsement, more than SOLOMON itself, emphasizes these effects.

4.3.3.4 Generating Resolution Tasks

Lastly, SOLOMON has encoded in LISP functions knowledge about how to generate resolution tasks. Uncertainty is viewed by SOLOMON as a problem to be solved, and endorsements as indicators or mnemonics for different kinds of problems. For example, if a proposition is endorsed as supported by inaccurate data, *and* SOLOMON establishes that this makes the proposition too uncertain to use in some other inference, then it has a "problem of inaccurate preconditions": What can it do to reduce its uncertainty? One strategy is to propose another task that may result in a corroboration between the desired proposition and another. SOLOMON uses inference rules to determine whether it has a problem and what kind of problem it is; the conclusions of these rules call LISP functions to fix the problem. These functions build new tasks, called resolution tasks, and place them on the agenda.

One of the major impediments to progress with SOLOMON has been its representations for knowledge. Much of SOLOMON's knowledge is embedded in LISP functions; for example, its knowledge about resolution tasks is *distributed* over a set of explicit rules that determine the kind of uncertainty that SOLOMON suffers, and a set of opaque functions that specify the remedy for the uncertainty. I am currently experimenting with the idea of including procedures for building resolution tasks in endorsements themselves, much as the **propmatch-if** and **rulematch-if** procedures are part of endorsements. Then an endorsement would say "Here is a reason to disbelieve a conclusion, but here is what you can do if you want to be more certain."

The following section discusses endorsements, the most important structures to SOLOMON's reasoning about uncertainty.

4.4 Endorsers and Endorsements

4.4.1 Rule Endorsements

Rule endorsements are associated with domain inference rules by the person who supplies the rules. Thus, they are specified a priori, and not generated in context by SOLOMON (see sections 4.4.2 and 4.4.3). Rule endorsements take the place of the initial numerical degrees of belief that are usually evoked from an expert when he or she produces an inference rule. My intention for rule endorsements is that they should provide a terminology to state reasons for especially trusting or mistrusting the conclusion of an inference rule. Said differently, I think there exists a relatively small number of relatively general things one might want to say about one´s confidence in a rule. One might comment on properties of the condition clauses, on the impact of the action, and on the *kind* of inference that the rule represents. For example, one might say that a condition of a rule is *maybe-too-general*, that the action is more *extreme* than the condition merits, and that the relationship between the condition and action is *correlational* -- that the state described in the condition co-occurs with that in the action. These rather general endorsements are available to any expert who uses SOLOMON; alternatively, that expert can design his or her own rule endorsements. Of course, in latter case, the expert must also specify how the new endorsements are to effect SOLOMON´s behavior.

4.4.1.1 Rule Condition Endorsements

When one specifies a domain rule in SOLOMON, individual clauses of the condition can be endorsed. The endorsements that follow are not exclusive and, thus, one might want to specify more than one for any given clause. This causes problems in the current version of SOLOMON because the system is unsure which of two or more **propmatch-if** and **rulematch-if** properties to use for a single clause (see section 4.4.1.3 for a discussion of these properties). In subsequent versions of

SOLOMON, this decision might be specified as part of the rule endorsement or inferred heuristically.

SOLOMON´s current corpus of rule condition endorsements is

1. **maybe-too-general**. More cases satisfy the condition than merit the conclusion. For example, in rule **RTI-1** (section 4.1) it is quite possible for someone to need lots of income and *not* have low tolerance for risk to income.

2. **maybe-too-specific**. Fewer cases satisfy the condition than merit the conclusion. For example, the condition **(age ?client high)** is usually too specific because many conclusions that hold for old people also hold for young people. Similarly, the condition of rule **RTI-1,** above, is **maybe-too-specific** as well as **maybe-too-general**.

3. **exact**. A catch-all notation whose interpretation is "there is no reason to mistrust this clause." I have used this endorsement when a condition clause is neither maybe-too-general, maybe-too-specific, nor a negation.

4. **supportive**. Supportive clauses are conjuncts that increase one´s confidence if true, but which do not necessarily cast doubt on the conclusion if false. For example, in the rule **(if (and (stated-risk-tolerance ?client low)(age ?client high)) then (risk-tolerance client low))**, the age clause is supportive. If a young client says he or she has low risk tolerance, one might still believe it.

5. **necessary**. Conceptually, the converse of **supportive**. Necessary clauses of a condition are those that must be believable for the rule to be used. For example, a necessary condition for recommending taxfree bonds is that the client have a high tax bracket.

6. **hard-not**. This specifies one of three interpretations of **not**. If a condition **(not (x))** is endorsed by hard-not, then **(not (x))** must appear in the database and be adequately endorsed, or a proposition mutually exclusive of **(x)** must appear in the database adequately endorsed, before the conclusion is believable.

7. **cwa**. cwa stands for the closed-world assumption, which is implicit in this endorsement. If a condition **(not(x))** is endorsed by cwa, then the conclusion is not believable unless **(not (x))** appears in the database and is adequately endorsed, *or* unless an attempt to prove **(x)** fails. Failure,

in SOLOMON, means that the result is not believable -- that it is inadequately endorsed.

8. **ostrich**. The weakest interpretation of **not**. If the condition **(not (x))** is endorsed by ostrich, then the conclusion is believable so long as **(x)** does not *currently* appear in the database.

9. **flexible**. A condition clause endorsed by flexible is believable if a proposition is found in the database that is equal or approximately equal to it, and this proposition is adequately endorsed.

10. **inflexible**. Some values must be precisely met or the condition clause becomes meaningless. For example, **(sex ?client female)** is not something that one should be uncertain about.

4.4.1.2 Discussion of Rule-condition Endorsements

I have been asked on a number of occasions why a system would accept and use rules that may be too general or too specific. One answer is that these rules might be nonetheless *useful*, but that they should be used with caution. Secondly, by identifying a rule as maybe too general or too specific, an expert provides a natural prompt to a knowledge acquisition system to start looking for additional rules. The task of a system that reasons about uncertainty is to mark overgenerality as a reason for mistrusting a rule´s conclusions, and if other evidence contrary to the conclusions becomes available, the system should use techniques peculiar to this negative endorsement, such as searching for corroboration, to resolve or discount its uncertainty.

There are numerous alternative ways to capture the intent of these rule condition endorsements. For example, the intent of labeling a clause **supportive** is satisfied by augmenting a single inference rule with another that lacks the supportive clause. Then, if the supportive clause is believable, the original rule fires and, if not, the other version fires. This seems a deficient scheme, though, because the intent of the supportive endorsement is that the supportive clause needn´t be believable, but this is implemented by a pair of rules, one of which requires the supportive clause to be believable and the other of which doesn´t mention it.

Similar concerns hold for the **flexible** endorsement. It is sometimes desirable to indicate that a rule´s condition need not be precisely met. One way to do this is to use inequalities; another is to make the condition disjunctive. For example, we may have condition **(age = old)**, or **(or (tax client low)(tax client medium))**. There is the problem, however, that our confidence in the condition may be related to how "definitely" the condition is met. For example, is someone old if their sixty-fifth birthday was last week? How about if the person is eighty-five years old? One may wish to specify a *credibility* distribution for a range of values, much as is done in the fuzzy-set approach for fuzzy predicates such as **old** (Gaines, 1976), and section 2.2.6. The flexible endorsement could easily specify a graded degree of belief depending on how well a datum satisfied a predicate; for example, if a client is 85 years old, the flexible endorsement would return a strong degree of belief that the client is old.[6]

But a word of caution pertains to using the flexible endorsement to implement fuzzy predicates. The difficulty is that, as with other endorsements, one´s belief in a proposition depends on what one wants to use the proposition for. Thus, the proper answer to the question above is that a person who turned 65 last week is unquestionably "old" for some purposes (e.g., social security payments), and less certainly "old" for other purposes (e.g., inferring general health). Thus, the attractive fuzzy set idea must be extended: The degree to which a person satisfies the predicate old depends on *more* than the person´s age. We agree that an 85-year old is more "old" than a 66-year old for the purpose of inferring the person´s health, but they may both be equally "over 65" for, say, social security purposes.

---

[6] I have not implemented this idea in SOLOMON because I have been eager to avoid degrees of belief; my goal has been to see how one can reason with structured symbolic reasons for believing, and introducing strengths of belief seems like a step backwards.

One of the more interesting aspects of the SOLOMON project has been reasoning about negations. The three endorsements **hard-not, cwa,** and **ostrich** are an attempt to distinguish the conditions under which one might believe **(not (x))**. The **ostrich** version appears to be too weak to be useful, but it is easy to imagine cases in which we are satisfied that **(x)** is false if it isn´t stated. McCarthy (1980), provides this humorous example:

> Imagine giving someone the [missionaries and cannibals] problem, and after he puzzles for a while, he suggests going upstream half a mile and crossing on a bridge. "What bridge," you say. "No bridge is mentioned in the statement of the problem." And this dunce replies, "Well, they don´t say there isn´t a bridge." You look at the English and even at the translation of the English into first order logic, and you must admit that "they don´t say" there is no bridge. (McCarthy, 1980, p. 30)

McCarthy´s explanation of why such dunce´s are rare is a mechanism "to conjecture that no relevant objects exist in certain categories except those whose existence follows from the statement of the problem and common sense knowledge." He calls the mechanism *circumscription*. The **ostrich** interpretation of **not** provides a mechanism similar to circumscription; one can ask "is **(not (location bridge upstream))** true," and conclude that it is because **(location bridge upstream)** is not explicitly stated.

The **cwa** interpretation of **not** says that **(not (location bridge upstream))** is believable if the **hard-not** interpretation (see below) is believable *or* if **(location bridge upstream)** is not believable. It thus corresponds to the THNOT operator (e.g., Winograd, 1980). The closed-world assumption is implicit in the endorsement, however, so the interpretation of a **cwa** endorsement of a proposition **(not (x))** is "I believe **(not (x))** because I can´t prove **(x)**, and if **(x)** was true I would be able to prove it." The final clause of this interpretation is the closed-world assumption.

Currently **cwa** and **non-cwa** endorsements of a clause **(not (x))** are ambiguous because they don´t distinguish between an attempt to prove **(x)** that returns **nil** -- which means that there are no rules to allow one to conclude **(x)** – and one that returns an inadequate endorsement. The former case means "**(x)** is not deducible," and the latter case means "**(x)** is not believable."

The interpretation of a **hard-not** endorsement of **(not (x))** is that the clause is believable if **(not (x))** appears in the database and is adequately endorsed, or if a proposition mutually exclusive of **(x)** is in the database and adequately endorsed. Checking the latter interpretation requires domain knowledge. For example, in FOLIO the client is asked about four possible objectives, of which some combinations are mutually exclusive. The objective of preserving capital is exclusive of the objective of growth, but growth is not exclusive of the objective of hedging against inflation.

There are currently five conditions under which **(not x)** can be inferred:

1. **x** may not exist in the database,
2. **x** may exist but be inadequately endorsed,
3. **(not x)** may be in the database and adequately endorsed,
4. something exclusive of **x** may be in the database and adequately endorsed, and
5. the attempt to prove **x** may simply fail.

The **ostrich-not** endorsement is satisfied with the first case, the **hard-not** endorsement with the third and fourth cases, and the **cwa-not** endorsement with all cases but the first. Clearly, there is considerable ambiguity about uncertainty in using the **hard-not** and **cwa-not** endorsements. SOLOMON´s corpus of endorsements of negations will have to be extended.

4.4.1.3 Propmatch-if and Rulematch-if for Rule Condition Endorsements

The **propmatch-if** and **rulematch-if** properties of rule condition endorsements contain procedures -- LISP lambda expressions. In a standard backward chaining program, a condition **(tax fred ?x)** is satisfied if there exists in the database a proposition that *unifies* with it. (See section 2.3.3.2 for an introduction to unification.) For example, if the database contains the proposition **(tax fred high)**, then the condition is satisfied. In SOLOMON, things are a little different. First, even if we find **(tax fred high)** in the database, we can not necessarily believe the condition **(tax fred ?x)**, because the proposition we found in the database might not be believable. Recall that in SOLOMON, presence of a proposition in the database does not imply that the proposition is "true," as it does in most predicate-calculus-based systems. But, for the purposes of explaining **propmatch-if** and **rulematch-if**, we will assume that if a proposition is found in the database, then it is adequately endorsed, and we will say that it "satisfies" the condition it matches. Thus, if we want to prove the condition **(tax fred ?x)**, then **(tax fred high)** is one proposition on the database that satisfies it. Now, imagine that we are trying to prove the condition **(not (age fred high))**. We would agree that it should suffice to find **(age fred low)** in the database. But **(age fred low)** does not unify with **(not (age fred high))**, which suggests that unification is not adequate to find all propositions in a database that satisfy a condition. However, the **propmatch-if** property specifies, for any clause in a condition, how to decide whether a proposition on the database satisfies the clause.

For example, the **propmatch-if** property for **hard-not** is:

```
'(lambda(clause prop)
        (or (unify-act clause prop)
            (conflict-clauses (cadr clause) prop)))
```

clause is a proposition of the form **(not (x))**, thus the **(cadr clause)** mentioned in the third line refers to propositions from which the **not** has been stripped. This **propmatch-if** property is a predicate that is embedded in a function that looks at each **prop** in the database in turn. For each **prop**, the function checks whether it unifies with **clause**, or whether **prop** conflicts with **(cadr clause)**.

For example, if **clause** is **(not (color ?object green))** (and the clause is endorsed by **hard-not**), then this **propmatch-if** might result in this list of propositions from the database: **(not (color hamburgers green)) (color roses red))**. Each of these propositions satisfies the clause, given that it is endorsed by **hard-not**.

Rulematch-if is very similar to **propmatch-if**. The main difference is that **rulematch-if** searches not in the database, but among rules. It´s job is to find rules whose conclusions match the clause we are currently trying to prove (assuming that we have not been able to find an adequately endorsed proposition in the database to match the clause). **Rulematch-if** is used in a function that returns a list of rules whose conclusions include the clause we want to prove. But just as with **propmatch-if**, we need not be limited to conclusions that unify with the clause. For example, rules that conclude **(color traffic-light red)** may be used to prove **(not (color traffic-light green))**

In summary, rule condition endorsements are a subset of the endorsements SOLOMON uses in place of initial degrees of belief in rules. Among these endorsements are rudimentary mechanisms to specify flexible or fuzzy predicates, and to decide when a proposition in the database or a rule´s conclusion matches a clause we want to prove.

A final comment on rule condition endorsements is that they seem to be few in number. This is an important result. It means that SOLOMON may be easily equipped to handle much of the uncertainty that is associated with inference rules. This should facilitate knowledge acquisition, since we may expect experts to prefer to recognize known problems in their rules than to generate their reasons for disbelieving a rule.

4.4.1.4 Rule Inference-type Endorsements

The basis for inferring a conclusion from its conditions is usually not explicit in AI programs. Yet, the kind of inference one makes affects one´s certainty in the conclusion and, thus, it seems appropriate to record the kind of inference in a rule endorsement. I will discuss three kinds of inference-type rule endorsements. Only one -- the *model-based* endorsement -- is implemented in SOLOMON. The other two are specializations of the model-based endorsement.

Three inference-type rule endorsements are

1. **model-based**. There is a principled explanation of why the state in the condition leads one to believe the state in the conclusion. This explanation, and particularly situations that would invalidate it, are part of the endorsement.

2. **causal**. The state described in the condition of the rule causes the state described in the rule´s action. For example, **(if high-income then high-tax)** is a causal inference, because high income causes high tax. A related endorsement is **reverse-causal**, which means that the state in a rule´s conclusion causes the state in the condition. Thus, the condition is an indication of the conclusion. For example, **(if (proportion stocks low) then (risk-tolerance low))** is a reverse causal relationship because low risk tolerance for principal causes a person to have a small proportion of stocks. The latter state is an indication of the former.

3. **correlational**. The state in the condition is associated with the state in the conclusion. For example, advanced age and low risk tolerance are associated, but it is difficult to discern a causal relationship between them.

An example of the use of the **model-based** endorsement is taken from a legal case of mistaken identity, recently presented on CBS´ "60 Minutes" program. A man was convicted of two counts of rape on the basis of eyewitness evidence. One can imagine an inference of the form **(if an eyewitness saw the defendant do something, then the defendent did it)**. The model that justifies this rule is that individuals do not look alike; thus, if a defendant is identified, then the defendant and no-one else is guilty. In the case presented by "60 Minutes," the defendant was *not* guilty (although he went to jail for about 5 years); the guilty person was another man of very similar appearance. In this bizarre case, one of the assumptions upon which an inference rule rests -- part of the model that justifies the rule and makes its conclusion believable -- was violated. The necessary conclusion in this case is that the inference of guilt is no longer believable.

Causal endorsements are just **model-based** endorsements for which the explanation of why the rule is credible is that the condition causes the conclusion (or vice versa). The interpretation of the **correlational** endorsement is that there might be a principled explanation of why the condition and conclusion are associated, but that we either don´t know it or don´t want to specify it. One slot of the correlational endorsement might be a strength of association -- a correlation -- between the condition and conclusion. I suspect that for expert systems, where many rules are "categorical" (Szolovits and Pauker, 1978) and used without reference to the theory that underlies them, the **correlational** endorsement is often appropriate. Moreover, it is possible that the degrees of belief typically associated with these rules are related in some way to the correlation between their conditions and conclusions.

However, for other model-based endorsements, and even for the **correlational** endorsement, one might want to use alternative methods to specify one´s confidence in the relationship between condition and conclusion. For example, Doyle (1983) suggests that inference rules may have the form $A \parallel B \Vdash C$, interpreted "A without B gives C." Thus, one may list the conditions under which one would be unwilling to conclude C, given A. This information, if known, is much more useful than a correlation or strength of association between a condition and conclusion. It is, for example, the kind of information we need to release from jail the man who was convicted for rape in the case of mistaken identity, above. We want to be able to say "if a defendant has been identified, and unless this individual looks like someone else, then the defendant is guilty as charged."

4.4.1.5 Conclusion Rule Endorsements

An inference rule consists of three components: A condition, some form of inference, and a conclusion. I have discussed endorsements of the condition and inference-type, but I have little to say about endorsements of conclusions. It is unclear what one can say about a conclusion, other than that it is (or is not) appropriate to the conditions and the type of inference that support it. While there may be little to say about the conclusions of inference rules, it is not the case for the conclusions of tasks: SOLOMON comments on relationships between a task conclusion and other conclusions that have been posted already (see section 4.4.3). For example, it may note a corroboration between an old conclusion and a newly posted one. Thus, while SOLOMON does not recognize endorsements of the conclusions of rules, it does recognize particular endorsements of conclusions of tasks.

4.4.2 Task Endorsements

Tasks are attempts to prove the conclusion of a rule. Section 4.5 discusses how tasks are generated. When SOLOMON puts a task on its agenda it generates for the task one of the following task endorsements:

1. **p-corroborate**. The conclusion of the task corroborates the conclusion of another task already on the agenda.

2. **p-conflict**. The conclusion of the task conflicts with the conclusion of another task on the agenda.

3. **p-potential-conflict**. The conclusion of the task may conflict with the conclusion of another task on the agenda.

4. **p-redundant**. The conclusion of the task is identical to the conclusion of another task that was derived from the same rule, and that has the same rule endorsement.

The conclusions of tasks are only "potential" conclusions, since they are not believable unless their conditions are believable. Thus, the prefix "p-" on the endorsements above. The interpretation of a **p-conflict** endorsement of two tasks, for example, is "if the condition of task 1 is believable and the condition of task

2 is believable, and both tasks are executed, then there will be a conflict between the conclusions of task 1 and task 2 when they are posted on the database."

The endorsement **p-potential-conflict** is used whenever SOLOMON cannot tell whether two conclusions are in conflict. For example, all would agree that **(risk-tolerance spencer low)** conflicts with **(risk-tolerance spencer high)**, but it is unclear which of these conflicts with **(risk-tolerance spencer (proportional income-need))**. Rather than evaluating **(proportional income-need)**, SOLOMON treats this latter conclusion as being in potential conflict with the other two.[7]

The **p-redundant** task endorsement arises from SOLOMON's method of handling disjunctive condition clauses (see 4.5). Briefly, a rule of the form **(if (or (x)(y)) then (z))** is broken into two tasks, **(if (x) then (z))** and **(if (y) then (z))**. These tasks each have the same rule endorsement -- which they inherit from the original task. The only difference between these tasks, then, is in their conditions. This situation is marked by endorsing the tasks as **redundant**. Should one succeed, there is no reason to execute another. Furthermore, SOLOMON is not permitted to execute two redundant tasks and then claim that their conclusions corroborate. This would be akin to saying "I believe a conclusion if X is believable *or* if Y is believable, and I believe it more if they are both believable." This is not an implausible statement, but in SOLOMON it should be made explicit by introducing another rule, identical to the first except with the disjunctive condition recast as a conjunctive.

4.4.3 Conclusion Endorsements

Conclusion endorsements mirror task endorsements, and are generated as conclusions are posted on the database. Four conclusion endorsements are

[7] Thus, potential conflict is a misnomer, because it might also imply potential corroboration.

corroborate, conflict, potential-conflict, and **redundant**.

In addition, there are a number of unimplemented conclusion endorsements that might refer to characteristics of conclusions. For example,

1. **unlikely**. We might note that a value in a conclusion is unusual or unlikely. For example, if a rule concludes that a client has a tax liability of less than 10%, we might endorse this as an **unlikely** conclusion.

2. **modal**. Conceptually the converse of **unlikely**.

3. **unwarranted.** Some rules may state stronger conclusions than are warranted by their conditions. For example, some assumptions -- such as, *unless the client says he´s in a low tax bracket, assume he´s in a high bracket* -- useful but not warranted. Saying that a conclusion is unwarranted is not to say that it should not be used. As always, we must decide whether a conclusion is endorsed *well-enough* for a particular purpose. But should two conclusions come into conflict, we might expect the one endorsed as unwarranted to be abandoned.

4.4.4 Data Endorsements

Data are supplied to SOLOMON at the outset of processing and endorsed by the person who supplies the data. Classes of data endorsements are

1. **source**. Where did the data come from? If it is supplied by a client it may be suspect; but if it is supplied by the Dow Jones wire services, it´s very likely to be accurate.

2. **type-of-data**. Some kinds of data provide one with better reasons to believe a conclusion than others. For example, two medical tests, both impeccably conducted, with an identical conclusion, may nonetheless support the conclusion to different degrees.

3. **accuracy**. Accuracy of data is a graded function (currently, low, medium, and high). However, this convention has been adopted primarily to illustrate SOLOMON´s abilities, and when a complete expert system is built in SOLOMON, with real data, on might would expect other characteristics of the data to gain preeminence over "accuracy."

4.4.5 Resolution Endorsements

When SOLOMON creates a task to resolve uncertainty, it also creates an endorsement for the task. Currently, these endorsements are mostly records of the type of resolution. They differ, however, from **conclusion-endorsements,** which include all the endorsements of the *conditions* of the conclusion, and thus, accrue huge numbers of endorsements to conclusions far down an inference chain (see section 4.4.6 on propagating endorsements.) When a chain of inference falters, and a resolution task is formed, the endorsement of the conclusion of the resolution task does not include those of its preconditions. This is a design decision that may well change in future implementations, but its justification is as follows: A resolution task is generated when no current task can produce a sufficiently certain conclusion. It´s interpretation is "You were stumped, but now you need not be," and so, the reasons that SOLOMON was "stumped" are not recorded, because they are in a sense irrelevant. This is almost certain to prove a bad method for keeping the number of endorsements accrued to a conclusion small. Other methods are discussed in the next section.

4.4.6 Propagating Endorsements over Inferences

Imagine an inference rule of the form **(if (and (a)(b)(c)) then (d))**. If **(a), (b)** and **(c)** are believable, then **(d)** should be believable, too, provided there is nothing incredible about the inference itself. On the other hand, if one or more of the premises of the inference are not trustworthy, then we might want to trust the conclusion less. In standard logic, this is not a problem, since one either does or does not believe the clauses in a premise, and the truth of a conjunction of clauses is easily derived from the truth of the individual clauses. Furthermore, if a premise is true, then the conclusion is also true. The situation is complicated in systems that use numerical degrees of belief. Now, the premise of a rule has a number associated with it, as does the rule itself, and these numbers are combined to produce a number for the conclusion. But if, instead of simple truth or degrees of belief, we substitute *reasons* for believing and disbelieving -- endorsements -- the question of what endorsements accrue to a conclusion becomes quite complicated.

SOLOMON currently uses a simple, default scheme for propagating endorsements, namely, all endorsements that arise in proving a task´s conclusion accrue to that conclusion. (An exception, for resolution endorsements was discussed in the previous section). Thus, the endorsements of the rule from which a task was derived, the task-endorsements of relationships (such as potential-conflict) among tasks on the agenda, the data-endorsements of data, and the conclusion endorsements of conclusions that that are used to prove the task´s conditions are all included in the endorsement of the conclusion of a task. Since conclusions are used to prove other tasks, SOLOMON builds up huge bodies of endorsements for conclusions after only a few inferences. Cumbersome though this is, its justification is simple: Any reasons for believing and disbelieving a premise are also reasons for believing and disbelieving the conclusion.

This principle may have heuristic power, but it is not obviously true for all inferences. It may be possible to reduce the corpus of endorsements where this principle fails. For example, consider the following rule:

```
(if    (and (goal ?client high-current-yield)
            (risk-tolerance ?client low))
 then (bond-need ?client high))
```

Imagine that the clause **(goal fred high-current-yield)** is in the database, and has been derived by three different rules, and each derivation is marred by some reason for disbelieving the conclusion. Under the default rule for propagating endorsements if we assert the conclusion **(bond-need fred high)**, we must also associate with it the three negative endorsements of the derivations of **(goal fred high-current-yield)**. However, an endorsement of each instance of **(goal fred high-current-yield)** is that it is corroborated with two other instances. Three separate derivations of the same conclusion, though individually untrustworthy, might together prove believable. If so, is there any reason to propagate the three negative endorsements of the premise **(goal fred high-current-yield)** to the conclusion **(bond-need fred high)**? This is an open question. I am not even sure how one goes about answering it; several possibilities are discussed next.

One might state principles of interaction between endorsements, such as "**corroboration** erases **low data accuracy**," and test the effects of these principles empirically. For example, if a rule´s conditional clause has been derived a number of ways, each from poor data, one need not mention the quality of the data in association with the rule´s conclusion. Another such principle might be that we can ignore poor endorsements of evidence for clauses endorsed as **supportive**. If these principles lead SOLOMON to believe conclusions that a human expert finds wanting, then they might be specialized, for example, to particular kinds of corroboration or supportive clauses.

Very general principles for propagating endorsements, that have relatively little to do with the identities of the endorsements, can also be formulated and tested as above. For example, we might keep just the most compelling endorsements, positive and negative, and ignore the rest. The liability of this approach is, of course, that endorsements may be more or less compelling in different contexts, so if we drop sound reasons for mistrusting a conclusion, and the reasons we have against it are irrelevant in a particular context, we may have lost the basis for rejecting the conclusion. Another possibility is that we try to *generalize* compelling endorsements. For example, imagine that The Big Bad Wolf asks for entrance to one Little Pig´s house, promising not to eat him. When admitted, the Wolf eats the Pig, of course, and goes on to the next Little Pig´s house. He again begs admittance and promises not to eat the owner, and when this Little Pig says, "That´s what you said about my brother," the Wolf replies "That was your brother, and hence, irrelevant." The Wolf might be right. The question is whether the Little Pig has overgeneralized his reason for mistrusting the Big Bad Wolf.

A third source of information about dropping endorsements might come from humans, in controlled psychological studies. We might test whether the Little Pig did indeed overgeneralize his negative endorsement. More importantly, we might test whether known errors, such as inattention to prior probabilities, might be modeled as inappropriate dropping of endorsements.

4.4.7 Ranking Endorsements

One of the attractive, and seductive, aspects of numerical degrees of belief is that one can rank uncertain alternatives. I say "seductive," because there may be no basis for the ranking other than that the alternatives have numbers attached to them. For example, imagine one has character-witness evidence that paints a glowing picture of a defendent, and eyewitness evidence from a drunkard pimp who says he saw the defendant commit a crime. Imagine that, by some method, one attaches degrees of belief to the evidence, that the character-witness evidence is preferred, and that the defendent is declared innocent. I would argue that this process is invalid, because the two kinds of evidence are not comparable. We may believe the character witnesses completely, but their evidence -- however credible -- cannot prove that the defendant did not commit the crime. Their evidence is literally irrelevant to that question. The evidence of the drunkard pimp, on the other hand, *can* prove the guilt of the defendant. The fact that the witness is not trustworthy may damn the prosecutor´s case, but we must be very careful to avoid saying "the character-witness testimony is reliable, and the drunkard's testimony isn't, thus the defendant is innocent."

It is both an advantage and a burden of the model of endorsement that viable comparisons of evidence have to be made explicit. The advantage is that we set the defendant above free for the *right* reason, namely, that the drunkard's evidence failed to prove the case beyond a reasonable doubt, as opposed to the *wrong* reason, that the testimony of the character-witnesses was more credible than that of the drunkard. The disadvantage is that we must, and do, specify all viable comparisons of evidence. For example, rule-endorsements are used to rank tasks on the agenda, and a small set of comparisons effect this ranking: Causal inferences are preferred to correlational ones. If no inference-type is specified, or if two tasks are of the same inference-type, rule condition endorsements are used to break the tie. Here, conditions that include clauses endorsed as **exact, necessary, inflexible,** and **hard-not** are preferred to those that include clauses endorsed as **maybe-too-general, maybe-too-specific, supportive,** and so on. Obviously, these are very rudimentary ranking criteria, but the endorsements themselves may be too general to support anything more principled.

In general, the problem of ranking endorsements might become very difficult. How does one rank a hypothesis with one strong positive endorsement and several weak negative ones against another hypothesis with several weak positive endorsements? The solution is related to the issue of propagating endorsements -- since one can only rank those endorsements that still exist after propagation -- and it is resolved just as simplistically. For the problem of ranking tasks according to their rule endorsements, as I noted, the criteria are very poor (see section 4.3.3.1).

4.4.8 The Meaning of Endorsements

Endorsements have operational semantics, by which I mean that their meaning is defined in terms of their effects on SOLOMON´s reasoning. Indeed, it was one of my design goals that knowledge about uncertain situations should actively affect SOLOMON´s behavior, so this seems an appropriate kind of semantics for endorsements. Three general components of the meaning of endorsements are

1. The situation in which the endorsement is accrued. For example, part of the meaning of the **p-corroborate** endorsement is that it applies whenever tasks on the agenda pending execution have corroborating conclusions.

2. The way that the endorsement interacts with *other* endorsements. For example, if we adopt a general principle that "**corroboration erases low data accuracy**," as was discussed in section 4.4.6, then I would consider this part of the meaning of **corroborate**.

3. The ranking of endorsements in different contexts. Despite my earlier comments that endorsements need not be ranked (see section 4.4.7), it must certainly count as part of the meaning of **corroborate**, for example, that it is a preferred endorsement to **contradict** -- that a conclusion that conflicts with another is less certain than one for which there is corroboration.

It would be very elegant if all endorsements of a particular type affected SOLOMON´s behavior in a characteristic way. This would help define a semantics for endorsements. For example, all rule endorsements are used for ranking tasks on the agenda, and all task endorsements either are used or can be used to generate resolution tasks. But beyond these simple regularities, the picture becomes muddy, especially for the rule condition endorsements (see section 4.4.1.1). For example, the three endorsements of clauses of the form **(not (x))** affect SOLOMON primarily via their **propmatch-if** and **rulematch-if** properties -- that is, by influencing the way SOLOMON searches for matching propositions in the database and the way it generates subgoals. The effect of the **maybe-too-general** endorsement, however, is felt primarily in the routine that decide whether a task contributes enough to SOLOMON´s certainty and by the routines that determine whether a proposition is believable in a particular context. Future implementations of SOLOMON may distinguish between these roles of rule condition endorsements and, thus, help to clean up the semantics of endorsements.

4.5 Control of processing in SOLOMON

At a very general level of description, SOLOMON´s control structure is that of a backward-chaining theorem-prover. Tasks have conditions and conclusions that are expressed in first-order logic. SOLOMON tries to prove the condition of a task and, if this fails, it generates ***subtasks*** that conclude some or all of the clauses in the condition of the original task. Then it tries to prove the conditions of the subtasks in exactly the same way as it attempted the conditions of the original task. This classic *hierarchical planning* approach is thoroughly discussed by Nilsson (1971, 1980), Cohen and Feigenbaum (1982, Chapter 15), Barr and Feigenbaum (1980, Chapter 2).

However, some assumptions that underly this simple approach do not hold in SOLOMON, and so SOLOMON´s control structure is more complicated. For example, it is assumed in the classic approach that the presence of a proposition in the problem-solver´s database is equivalent to asserting the truth of the proposition. Thus, the condition of a rule is met if a proposition is found in the database to match it. In SOLOMON, the credibility of a proposition varies with the evidence it accrues and the purposes for which it is to be used. This means that finding a proposition in the database to match a condition is no guarantee that the condition is satisfied.

SOLOMON´s control is managed primarily by the two functions shown in Figure 4-1. Rather than explain each line-by-line, I will present two examples of

SOLOMON at work. I will take lengthy detours from these traces of SOLOMON, to explain how it achieves its results.

```
(defun run-tasks ()
      loop
      (cond((setq c-task (dequeue task-db))
             (cond((task-endorsed-ok c-task)
                    (or (run-task c-task)
                        (subtasks-for c-task)
                        (propose-task-resolution c-task)))
                   (t (propose-task-resolution c-task)))
             (go loop))
            (t nil)))


(defun run-task (task)
      (let*((condition (get-val task ´condition))
            (action   (get-val task ´action))
            (condition-end-ok (wff-endorsed-ok condition prop-db))
            (action-end-ok nil)
            (parent (get-val task ´parent-task))
            (parent-condition
                    (and parent (get-val parent ´condition))))

            (assert task condition-end-ok)

            (setq action-end-ok (wff-endorsed-ok action prop-db))

           (cond((and (or (eq (car action-end-ok) ´good)
                            (eq (car condition-end-ok) ´good))
                        parent
                        (task-endorsed-ok parent))
                  (setq c-task parent)
                  (run-task parent))

                 ((eq (car condition-end-ok) ´bad)
                  (propose-task-resolution task))

                 (t nil))
            )))
```

Figure 4-1: The control functions **run-tasks** and **run task**

There are three global entities in this structure: Task-db is SOLOMON´s agenda of tasks; prop-db is its database, on which all data and conclusions are posted; and, c-task is a global variable set to the identifying number of the current task. The function **run-tasks** iterates until it runs out of tasks. First, it **dequeues** a task from task-db, and gives its number to c-task. Then it asks if the task is adequately endorsed. If so, it tries to run the task. If this fails, it tries to propose subtasks for the task. Then, if it is unable to generate any subtasks by conventional means, *this* fails, it calls **propose-task-resolution** to propose an alternative task. Similarly, if **task-endorsed-ok** indicates that the task lacks an adequate endorsement, **propose-task-resolution** is called to suggest an alternative task. I will describe each of these steps in detail in the following examples.

4.5.1 SOLOMON´s Control Structure: Example 1

SOLOMON´s task in this example is to find credible evidence for the proposition **(risk-tolerance spencer low)**. The first attempt to find a proposition on prop-db that matches this goal fails:

Task-db = (nil)
Enter run-task. Task = task-00015
Condition = (risk-tolerance spencer low)
Action = (finished problem)
On db? = nil

Deciding that a clause is adeuqately endorsed. These are the details of how SOLOMON concludes that no proposition in prop-db matches **(risk-tolerance spencer low)**. First, the function **wff-endorsed-ok** is called on this condition. **wff-endorsed-ok** asks whether each clause in the condition is **prop-endorsed-ok**, and combines the results according to the logical structure of the condition. This will be explained further, shortly. **prop-endorsed-ok** looks at individual clauses, such as **(size elephant large)** and returns one of three things. It returns **(good datum-00017)** if it finds a datum called **datum-00017** that matches **(size elephant large)**, *and* if **datum-00017** is adequately endorsed.[8] That is, **prop-endorsed-ok** returns the name of the *first* proposition on prop-db that satisfies its argument. Second, it may return a list of the form **(bad datum-00021 conc-00231)** if **datum-00021** and **conc-00231** match **(size elephant large)** but are *in*adequately endorsed. That is, it returns the list of all matching but non-believable propositions. Thirdly, **prop-endorsed-ok** returns **nil** if it fails to find a proposition on prop-db to match **(size elephant large)**. This is what happened with the condition of **task-00015**, above.

wff-endorsed-ok combines the results of calling **prop-endorsed-ok** on the clauses in a task´s condition. That is, **(wff-endorsed-ok ´(and (P a b)(Q c d)))** returns **(good datum-00174 datum-01001)** if **(prop-endorsed-ok ´(P a b))** returns **(good datum-000174)** and **(prop-endorsed-ok ´(Q c d))** returns **(good datum-01001))**. If **(prop-endorsed-ok ´(P a b))** is **(bad datum-00921)** or **nil**, then **wff-endorsed-ok** will return **(bad datum-00921)** or **nil**, regardless of the result of calling **prop-endorsed-ok** on the other clause.

Generating subtasks. At this point in the example, SOLOMON has tried to prove the condition of **task-00015** but failed. It now generates *subtasks*. These are new tasks whose conclusions match the condition of **task-00015**. Matching for rules can be by ordinary unification or by something fancier, as discussed above and in section 4.4.1.3. SOLOMON finds three tasks that conclude **(risk-tolerance spencer low)**. They are put on task-db in an order determined by their rule-endorsements. Those tasks that have strong positive rule endorsements are placed on task-db ahead of tasks with lesser endorsements. As it happens, the three tasks that are generated for the goal **(risk-tolerance spencer low)** are equally poorly endorsed, so they are put on task-db in the order in which they are generated:

Task-db = (task-00038 task-00040 task-00045)

---

[8] As we discussed in section 4.4.1.3, rule endorsements specify a variety of matching criteria. The default method is unification (see section 2.3.3.2), but more sophisticated methods are available.

Screening tasks. The next step is to try to prove one of these tasks´ conditions. First, **task-00038** is dequeued from task-db. But before it is executed, it is screened by the function **task-endorsed-ok**. **Task-endorsed-ok** returns **nil** if there is a reason not to execute the task, and **t** otherwise. The purpose of **task-endorsed-ok** is to filter out tasks that do not contribute to SOLOMON´s certainty of a hypothesis. **Task-endorsed-ok** is sensitive to context; that is, it will accept a task as adequately endorsed for some purposes but not for others. For example, if SOLOMON is trying to prove a clause that is endorsed as **supportive** or **flexible** (see section 4.4.1.1), then it will accept a task with almost any endorsement. On the other hand, if it is trying to prove a clause endorsed as **necessary**, then it will reject tasks endorsed as having **maybe-too-general** conditions.[9]

In this example, **task-00038** gets the go-ahead, and SOLOMON now tries to prove its condition:

```
Task-db =(task-00040 task-00045)
Enter run-task. Task = task-00038
Condition = (srt-interest spencer low)
Action = (risk-tolerance spencer low)
On db? = (bad datum-00020)

The endorsements of the preconditions:
(bad datum-00020)

Endorsement data-end-00021.
(data-type ((= . interview))
data-accuracy ((= . low)))
```

SOLOMON does indeed find a proposition on prop-db that matches the condition **(srt-interest spencer low)**. To do so it uses the functions **wff-endorsed-ok** and **prop-endorsed-ok**, described above. Unfortunately, the datum is not adequately

[9] This rule is admittedly stringent, and is included primarily to illustrate the possibility of context-dependent filtering of tasks.

endorsed. Its endorsement includes **(data-accuracy = low)**, which is too poor an endorsement to support **task-00038**.

Asserting conclusions. Despite the inadequate endorsement of the condition of task-00038, its conclusion is asserted:

Asserting (risk-tolerance spencer low)

This strategy is significantly different from that of standard theorem provers, for which the presence of a proposition in a database is interpreted to mean that the proposition is *true*. In SOLOMON, there are no true or false propositions, but all propositions have associated endorsements -- reasons to believe and disbelieve them. Even if the condition of a rule is inadequately endorsed, its conclusion is put onto prop-db. There, the conclusion can function in one or more of three ways.

1. A conclusion **(risk-tolerance spencer low)**, whose condition is inadequately endorsed, may satisfy the clause **(not (risk-tolerance spencer low))** (see section 4.4.1.1).

2. The conclusion undergoes the process of **conclusion endorsement** when it is asserted, and this may well change its status from not credible to believable. For example, if the conclusion corroborates another, the credibility of each increases, even though neither may have support from their conditions. This is why, in Figure 4-1, **run-task** sets **action-end-ok** to the result of running **wff-endorsed-ok** on a newly asserted conclusion.

3. A poorly endorsed proposition may be considered useful for some later task, even if it is inadequate for the current one. Thus, all conclusions should be posted, regardless of their endorsements.

Although SOLOMON asserts the conclusion **(risk-tolerance spencer low)**, it knows there is no point to returning to the *parent task*, **task-00015**, because the conclusion does not have adequate support. This is shown in the last few lines of code in the function **run-task** (Fig. 4-1). Instead, it tries to **propose-task-resolution** for this conclusion -- that is, to find some task that will increase the support for the conclusion:

```
I cannot prove the goal because (datum-00020)
are inadequately endorsed. Trying to find a resolution.
```

SOLOMON has a number of heuristics for proposing task resolutions, but let us assume that none applies here, so it returns to the tasks on task-db and tries to prove the next one:

```
In Task-endorsed-ok. Task = task-00040
Task is to prove = (risk-tolerance spencer low)
task-00040 is adequately endorsed.

Task-db =(task-00045)
Enter run-task. Task = task-00040
Condition = (income-need spencer high)
Action = (risk-tolerance spencer low)
On db? = (bad datum-00026)

The endorsements of the preconditions:

(bad datum-00026)

Endorsement data-end-00027.
        (data-type ((= . interview))
         data-accuracy ((= . low)))

Asserting (risk-tolerance spencer low)
```

Resolving uncertainty with conclusion endorsements. We have seen this kind of problem before: SOLOMON finds a datum to match a conditional clause, but the datum is poorly endorsed. Once again, SOLOMON asserts the clause **(risk-tolerance spencer low)**. But note that this time it does not search for a resolution task to provide better support for **(risk-tolerance spencer low)**, as it did after task-00038. This is because it believes it has strong enough support now: Even though neither individual instance of **(risk-tolerance spencer low)** has the support of its condition, SOLOMON discovers that the conclusions support each other by corroboration. Following are parts of the endorsements of **conc-00048** and

conc-00053, the frames that resulted from twice asserting **(risk-tolerance spencer low)**:

```
conc-00048:
    Endorsement data-end-00021.
            (data-type ((= . interview))
             data-accuracy ((= . low)))
    Endorsement conc-end-00054.
            (corroborate ((prop conc-00048 conc-00053)))

conc-00053:
    Endorsement data-end-00027.
            (data-type ((= . interview))
             data-accuracy ((= . low)))
    Endorsement conc-end-00055.
            (corroborate ((prop conc-00048 conc-00053)))
```

Summary. SOLOMON is now convinced that **(risk-tolerance spencer low)**, so its problem is solved. This example illustrated several aspects of SOLOMON´s control structure: First, when SOLOMON want to prove a proposition, it cannot assume that the presence of that proposition in its database is equivalent to the proposition being *true*. Instead, if it wants to prove **(P a b)**, the functions **wff-endorsed-ok** and **prop-endorsed-ok** return a **(good ...)** list of the first adequately endorsed proposition in prop-db that matches **(P a b)**, or a **(bad...)** list of all the propositions in prop-db that match **(P a b)** but that are inadequately endorsed, or **nil** if no propositions in prop-db match **(P a b)**. Secondly, SOLOMON allows for different interpretations of what it means for propositions to *match*. The default is simple unification, but the endorsements of clauses can also specify procedures to effect matches (see 4.4.1.3). Third, SOLOMON always asserts the conclusions of tasks it performs, even if the conditions of the tasks lack adequate endorsement. These conclusions can nonetheless be useful to SOLOMON in later processing. This was illustrated when SOLOMON found a corroboration between **conc-00048**, whose condition lacked proper endorsement, and **conc-00053**, which also lacked support. Although neither of these conclusions was supported by an adequately endorsed condition, their mutual corroborative support was conclusive for SOLOMON. Fourth, SOLOMON screens tasks before performing them to ensure that a task that looked promising when it was scheduled still holds promise.

The following example illustrates how SOLOMON resolves uncertainty by generating resolution tasks.

4.5.2 SOLOMON´s Control Structure: Example 2

SOLOMON´s goal in this example is to prove

(and (tax fred high)
(income-need fred low))

from which it can conclude **(taxable-bond-need fred low)**. Relevant facts are

(tax fred high) is already on prop-db and adequately endorsed.

the rule-endorsement of **(income-need fred low) is **(supportive)**.

SOLOMON generates a task, **task-00016**, with the condition and conclusion as just described, checks with **task-endorsed-ok** whether the task should be run, and passes the task´s condition to **wff-endorsed-ok**. This function returns **(bad datum-00013)**, because **datum-00013** does indeed state that **(income-need fred low)**, but, it is endorsed as a datum with low data accuracy. Thus, even though SOLOMON knows **(tax fred high)** is adequately endorsed, the union of the two clauses is not well-supported.:

Task-db =(nil)
Enter run-task. Task = task-00016
Condition = (and (tax fred high) (income-need fred low))
Action = (taxable-bond-need fred low)
On db? = (bad datum-00013)

The endorsements of the preconditions (bad datum-00013):

Endorsement data-end-00014.
(data-type ((= . interview))
data-accuracy ((= . low)))

Asserting (taxable-bond-need fred low)

But, as always, the conclusion of a rule is asserted even if its conditions are not adequately endorsed. SOLOMON tries now to find a task that will provide better support for **(taxable-bond-need fred low)**. It reasons that since the failed clause of **task-00016** was endorsed as **(supportive)**, it is not *required* to be believable for the conclusion of **task-00016** to be believable. SOLOMON proposes an alternative task, **res-00019**, that lacks the clause **(income-need fred low)**. It then checks **res-00019** with **task-endorsed-ok**, and executes it:

I cannot prove the goal because (datum-00013)
are inadequately endorsed. Trying to find a resolution.

In Task-endorsed-ok. Task = res-00019
Task is to prove = (taxable-bond-need fred low)
res-00019 is adequately endorsed.

Task-db =(nil)
Enter run-task. Task = res-00019
Condition = (and (tax fred high))
Action = (taxable-bond-need fred low)
On db? = (good datum-00010)

The endorsements of the preconditions (good datum-00010):

Endorsement data-end-00011.
(data-type ((= . interview))
data-accuracy ((= . medium)))

Asserting (taxable-bond-need fred low)

Note that **res-00019** is just **task-00016** with the supportive (and inadequately endorsed) clause **(income-need fred low)** dropped. The function that generates this and all resolution tasks is called **propose-task-resolution**. It is called whenever the task that has just been popped from task-db is inadequately endorsed, and SOLOMON can find no viable subtasks for it (see Fig. 4-1, **run-tasks**); or when a task´s condition accrues a **(bad...)** endorsement from **wff-endorsed-ok** (see Fig. 4-1, near the bottom of **run-task**).

Resolution tasks, unlike regular tasks, are not put on task-db in an order determined by their rule endorsements, but rather, are pushed onto the front of task-db and executed in a FIFO order. The reason is that in both cases in which a resolution task is proposed, SOLOMON really needs to come up with a resolution to its uncertainty immediately. In the first case, when a task is popped from task-db but fails **task-endorsed-ok**, there is little point to trying another task because we already know that the failed task has the best a priori rule-endorsements of all the tasks on the agenda. After all, tasks are ranked by their rule endorsements on the agenda. In the second case, where a task´s condition lacks adequate endorsement, it is best to execute a resolution task before any other because there is no guarantee that other tasks on task-db have any pertinence to the failed task.

SOLOMON has, at this point dropped the supportive clause from its original task, and successfully proved the condition and asserted the conclusion of the resolution task. Its problem, or rather a variant of it, is now solved. Note, however, that the endorsement of its conclusion is not entirely without blemish: **res-00019** has picked up a **maybe-too-general** endorsement. This is because it was produced by dropping a supportive clause from the condition of **task-00016**, but maintaining its conclusion. Thus, the condition is maybe-too-general for the conclusion:

```
Condition            : (and (tax fred high))
Action               : (taxable-bond-need fred low)
Motive for task      : (taxable-bond-need fred ?x)
From domain rule     : i-taxablebond-need1
Parent task          : starter

     ...

Endorsement res-end-00020.
      (original-task ((= . task-00016)))

      ...

Endorsement res-end-00022.
     (isa (( = . maybe-too-general-00023)))

     ...
```

This example illustrated SOLOMON's ability to generate new tasks, called resolutions, to run when conventionally-derived tasks fail to provide well-endorsed conclusions. This is one of SOLOMON's most interesting abilities, suggesting that even when we are uncertain of a result, we still know much about the result that can be helpful to decreasing our uncertainty.

This concludes the discussion of the current model of endorsement and the current implementation of SOLOMON. Much work remains before SOLOMON has the utility of, say, EMYCIN. Like EMYCIN, SOLOMON abstracts some basic AI principles, notably the backward chaining control structure and the separation of knowledge from control. But the model of endorsement is novel, and much remains to be done to prove its power. The next chapter is a discussion of the issues involved in bringing the model of endorsement to maturity.

5 Future Research

5.1 Introduction

The endorsement-based approach to uncertainty outlined in these chapters is potentially very powerful. If it delivers what it promises, then researchers in AI will have a tool for representing and reasoning about uncertain situations, a rich vocabulary for expressing reasons for believing and disbelieving, an architecture for the heuristic weighing and propogation of endorsements, and the ability to extend reasoning about uncertainty to discounting and resolving uncertainty. The SOLOMON program currently has all these abilities, but it is a small system. My immediate goal for the future is to show that the basic ideas of the model of endorsement work well for large systems developed in the SOLOMON framework. This chapter discusses the developments that I anticipate will facilitate scaling up SOLOMON, and the likely benefits of the endorsement-based approach. We start with a discussion of the contributions of the endorsement idea and SOLOMON, then turn to inadequacies of SOLOMON, and then discuss how SOLOMON and the model of endorsement might be evaluated.

Since this document was first drafted, but prior to this version, research in the model of endorsement has been focused on the related problems of specifying combination mechanisms and semantics for endorsements. I have added a section at the end of this Chapter that represents some of this work. It answers some of the questions asked in the original sections of the Chapter, but I have resisted the temptation to revise these sections in light of my current research. Rather, I wish to make it clear that Sections 5.2, 5.3, and 5.4 are as they were originally written in August of 1983; Section 5.5 was drafted in June of 1984.

5.2 Analysis of the Endorsement-based Approach

5.2.1 The Contribution of this Research

The model of endorsement is an artificial intelligence approach to reasoning about uncertainty. It is based on the idea that we have *reasons*, called endorsements, for believing and disbelieving hypotheses and that these can be used to weigh evidence, to model changes in beliefs over inferences, to decide whether a result is certain enough to be used in subsequent reasoning, to represent evidential relationships (such as contradiction) between conclusions, and to design new tasks with the goal of decreasing uncertainty. Endorsements facilitate reasoning *about* uncertainty, in contrast with non-reflective, algorithmic approaches such as are commonly used in AI programs today. The model shows how an AI system that solves problems by successive inferences can manage the uncertainty that is introduced by poor data, assumptions, conflicting conclusions, and the inference rules themselves. The model is implemented in a computer program called SOLOMON, which is intended as a demonstration of these ideas and, ultimately, and a tool for building AI systems that reason about uncertainty.

A positive outcome of this work is its emphasis that theories of uncertainty are *tools* for representing and reasoning about uncertainty. This leads naturally to a set of evaluation criteria for this work and other approaches. We can specify what it means for tools to be useful, and ask how they stack up against each other. Sections 3.3 and 3.5 compare the endorsement-based approach with a Bayesian model. Each is shown to have distinct advantages and disadvantages; principal among the disadvantages of the endorsement-based approach is the difficulty of expressing *degree* or *strength* of belief. This will be discussed further in the next section. I mention it here as an example of the kind of comparisons that follow the decision to treat theories of uncertainty as representational tools.

A general and, I think, important contribution is to view uncertainty in terms of its effects on problem solving behavior. This orientation permeates the SOLOMON program, but a specific and promising consequence is the ability to propose resolution tasks (see section 4.3.3). I have been struck, throughout this research, by the human ability to act decisively in the face of uncertainty. We find ways to discount or resolve uncertainty, whether by assumption, inquiry, hedging, worst-case analysis, buying insurance, or the simple expedient of "wait and see." We rarely find humans carrying around psychologically taxing bodies of fears, anxieties, and uncertainties. Only in very extreme cases are humans paralysed by indecision; almost invariably we are able to act. Part of this ability has to do with the environment, since it rarely confronts us with yes-or-no decisions without the option of gathering more information. But we still need to know how to obtain the information. Resolution tasks in the SOLOMON system are the product of SOLOMON's knowledge about what to do when it is too uncertain to make a decision. This situation of uncertainty is summarized in one or more endorsements, which SOLOMON views as a statement of a problem: "I am uncertain, this is why -- , do something about it." I anticipate that the ability to propose resolution tasks will be one of the major benefits of the endorsement-based approach.

5.3 Problems with SOLOMON

SOLOMON left some basic problems unsolved. It was easy to finesse them because SOLOMON is a small prototype program. For example, the default rule for propagating endorsements over inferences (to propagate *all* endorsements of preconditions -- see section 4.4.6), results in long lists of endorsements for conclusions after just a few inferences. I expect that this will become unmanagable as SOLOMON scales up.

SOLOMON is a small system for two reasons. First, the FOLIO program that is used as a testbed bases its conclusions on single-step inferences. Client parameters, such as risk-tolerance, are assumed by FOLIO to be certain, because the rules I derived from Mark Lieberman (the domain expert) are those he applies *after* establishing these characteristics to his satisfaction. It was not until late in the FOLIO project that I was able to arrive at rules for establishing risk tolerance -- such as **if the client currently has few stocks then the client has low risk tolerance** -- and other client parameters.[1] Not only was it difficult to derive these rules, but also it was not easy to determine a set of domain-specific endorsements. The chief reason, it appears, for mistrusting evidence of risk tolerance or some other parameter, is inconsistencies between pieces of evidence (including preconceptions). And the chief strategy for resolving this uncertainty seems to be to ask more questions. In summary, the FOLIO domain seems after all to involve very short inference chains, and very simple approaches to uncertainty. It has thus limited the expansion of SOLOMON.

The other reason that SOLOMON remains a prototype is the need to redesign its knowledge representations. Currently, endorsements are represented as frames, and pertinent and peculiar actions are procedural attachments to the frames. For example, the frame for the **flexible** endorsement includes a peculiar **propmatch-if** procedure that allows approximate matches, and children of this frame -- specializations of the **flexible** endorsement -- may carry specialized matching criteria. However, a number of procedures that should be attached to individual endorsements currently float around in functions in SOLOMON. Three general functions that will be discussed shortly are proposing resolution tasks, propagating endorsements over inferences, and ranking endorsements. There are several reasons to associate these functions with individual endorsements. First, the semantics of endorsements are operational -- the meaning of an endorsement is how it makes SOLOMON behave. We want the functions that implement these behaviors to be

[1] And I am not convinced that these rules capture Mr. Lieberman's reasoning; his determination of these parameters seems much more a perceptual, intuitive process than a reasoning one.

immediately associated with the endorsements, so that by looking at an endorsement we can see how it affects behavior. Secondly, if it is obvious how extant, general endorsements affect behavior, then this information can be used to build new endorsements. We can adopt Randy Davis's (1976) approach from TEIRESIAS and have general "endorsement frames" to guide the acquisition of new endorsements. Finally, we can exploit the hierarchical structure of endorsements to index resolution methods of more or less generality.

Procedures to design resolution tasks should ideally be attached to endorsements. For example, the **conflict** endorsement should advise SOLOMON to 1) search for a conclusion corroborating one of the conflicting propositions, or 2) diversify over the alternatives; the **conflict of possession** endorsement should advise the system to divide the contested goods between the contestants; and the **conflict of possession over a living thing** endorsement should award custody to one contestant and visiting hours to the other. Since resolutions become more specific as endorsements do, it makes sense to exploit the hierarchical structure of endorsements to organize resolution methods. This kind of organization illustrates how King Solomon might have ordered the baby cut in two: If he lacked a resolution method for uncertainty about possession of children, he might easily have inherited a default method -- such as, dividing the contended possession in half -- from a more general and inapplicable endorsement.

Two other general functions that should probably be attached to individual endorsements are ranking endorsements and propagating them over inferences. In the first case, we have at least general knowledge about how endorsements stack up against one another: The **corroboration** endorsement might include the fact that corroboration is preferable to contradiction. Each endorsement may carry lists of inferior and superior endorsements from which to construct a partial ordering over endorsements. Similarly, endorsements might carry information that will help with the propagation problem; for example, the **low data accuracy** endorsement might specify, "If you find corroborating evidence, then I become irrelevant." This information could then be used to drop the **low data accuracy** endorsement from a body of endorsements that include **corroboration**.

In summary, the endorsement-based approach and SOLOMON in particular are nascent and promising. Two major problems are that the original domain of portfolio management does not afford the opportunities for reasoning about uncertainty that are needed to exercise the system, and the system´s knowledge needs reorganizing so that one can more easily understand the effects of endorsements, and thus, their meaning. The next section addresses the latter problem again by looking at resolution, propagation, and ranking in more detail. The following section raises the issue of SOLOMON´s test domain again in the context of a evaluating the program.

5.3.1 Resolution, Propagation, and Ranking

When SOLOMON is dissatisfied with the endorsement of a conclusion, or when it cannot find an agenda task that is adequately endorsed, it tries to generate a *resolution task* (see section 4.5.2). When SOLOMON derives a conclusion, it must determine the conclusion´s endorsement; and, if the preconditions are uncertain then some characterization of this uncertainty must *propagate* over the inference, from the endorsement of the precondition to the endorsement of the conclusion. When SOLOMON is scheduling tasks on its agenda, it does so by *ranking* the tasks´ rule endorsements. Similarly, when weighing evidence to decide which of several propositions is most believable, it must rank endorsements (see section 4.4.7). The first of these abilities -- to generate resolution tasks -- is novel to AI approaches to uncertainty. The other two abilities seem obviously necessary, and are found in all the approaches to uncertainty described in Chapter 2.

Resolving Uncertainty. There are two general kinds of resolution tasks, those that reduce or remove uncertainty, and those that permit one to ignore the uncertainty temporarily. A case of the first kind, of *resolving* uncertainty, might involve asking for some missing information: I am uncertain who won the Superbowl last year so I ask someone who knows. A case of the second kind, which I call *discounting* uncertainty, is diversifying one's investments: I am uncertain whether interest rates will go up and send the stock market down, or vice versa, so I buy stocks and moneymarket funds that, in concert, minimize the negative (and necessarily the positive) impact of either eventuality. Resolutions of uncertainty may *not* result in certainty; for example, in the Superbowl case we simply trade uncertainty about our own knowledge for (hopefully lesser) uncertainty about the knowledge of the person we consult. Indeed, it is interesting to speculate whether so-called resolutions of uncertainty *ever* eliminate uncertainty entirely, or whether they simply reduce it to an acceptable level. In any case, resolving uncertainty seems qualitatively different from discounting it – from minimizing the impact of the uncertainty but not the uncertainty itself. These cases are not distinguished by SOLOMON, but it seems evident that they should be. Currently, SOLOMON treats any resolution task as producing an adequately endorsed conclusion, and ignores the question of whether uncertainty has been eliminated or just suspended.

This is not the only distinction between resolution tasks that SOLOMON fails to make. The program will not, for example, differentiate between a corroboration of one poorly-endorsed and one well-endorsed hypothesis, and a corroboration of two poorly endorsed hypotheses. It seems that SOLOMON ought to recognize the former as more certain than the latter, but it does not. In fact, the endorsements of resolution tasks are inadequate; SOLOMON treats a resolution task as "certain enough," and does not endorse it further. Obviously, there is room for improvement on this scheme.

The idea of treating uncertainty as a problem and a resolution task as a solution is potentially very powerful and it should be extended beyond its current implementation. One area of improvement is to resolve uncertainty by experiment. Currently, all resolution tasks are based on information available at the time.

Clearly, there is much to be gained by giving SOLOMON the ability to reason about *unavailable* information. For example, SOLOMON might ask whether more evidence *could* be had, whether it is worth the effort of getting it, how to get it, and so on.

Propagating Endorsements. A potentially limiting factor for the model of endorsement is the proliferation of endorsements as SOLOMON reasons. Currently, a conclusion accrues endorsements from the preconditions of an inference, from any data that might be used to prove a precondition, from the inference rule itself, and from evidential relationships (such as conflict) between the conclusion and others in SOLOMON's database. Of these, the first contributes most to the proliferation of endorsements. Obviously, some record of the trustworthiness of each precondition must be associated with the conclusion; the question is whether *all* endorsements of *all* preconditions must automatically be associated with their conclusion. Some devices to reduce this information load are dropping endorsements and replacing endorsements when they appear in particular combinations. For example, we might drop all but the best and the worst of a conclusion's endorsements, or we might drop all endorsements that are more than two or three inferences old (i.e., originally associated with earlier conclusions), or we might drop all endorsements except those for resolution tasks. Similarly, we might replace a body of endorsements that, in concert, form a meaningful whole, with a single endorsement.

Clearly, there is much to be learned empirically about propagation of endorsements. The main observation about this problem, however, is that a careful balance must be maintained between dropping so much information that intelligent processing ceases, and keeping so much information that intelligent processing collapses under its weight.

Ranking Endorsements. At first glance it appears that any theory of uncertainty requires a method to tell which of two propositions is the most certain.

In numerical and control approaches, this is managed by a number, since numbers are easily compared for magnitude. In the model of endorsement, these comparisons are qualitative, not quantitative. We ask whether endorsement **A** is preferred to endorsement **B**, and, with more sophistication, whether a body of several endorsements $\mathbf{e_A}$ is preferred to another set $\mathbf{e_B}$. But one of the surprises of the SOLOMON project is that this ability is not "obviously" necessary. SOLOMON uses it rarely and could probably not use it at all.

SOLOMON ranks endorsements only when it schedules tasks on its agenda and, in theory, to resolve conflicts between hypotheses. In theory, if **P = (size box-1 large)** and **Q = (size box-1 small)**, then we can determine which proposition is most certain by ranking the endorsements of **P** and **Q**. This has not been implemented in SOLOMON, although a simple endorsement-ranking algorithm is discussed in section 4.3.3.1. We are inclined to think of ranking endorsements as the only way to break the impasse formed by contradictory hypotheses, but, in fact, there are many other methods. We might average the values and conclude that box-1 is a "medium size." If the difference in size is small, or unimportant, we might choose arbitrarily. We might "hedge our bets," and commit ourselves to neither hypothesis. For example, if we needed a bag in which to carry box-1, we might buy two bags, one small and one large. Or, a "worst-case analysis" suggests buying a single, large bag. Each of these approaches is easily managed in SOLOMON by resolution tasks. The issue they raise is, if there are other ways to resolve uncertainty besides taking the best endorsed alternative, is it necessary to rank endorsements? Quite possibly, we can do without this ability, at least for resolving conflicts. In practice, though, choosing the most certain (best-endorsed) alternative may be the *simplest* way to resolve a conflict. Furthermore, we must still rank endorsements to schedule tasks on SOLOMON's agenda.

But consider the issue more closely: If the *only* use for ranking endorsements was to resolve between conflicting and unequally endorsed hypotheses, would it be worth the effort to specify ranking criteria for all endorsements. This is a far more difficult task that simply comparing two numbers with the $\geq$ operator. We must ask how often hypotheses conflict in nature. How often do we find, say, simultaneous and passably credible claims that a person´s risk tolerance is both high and low? How often are we actually required to *weigh* evidence? In the examples of Chapter 3, we noted that Walker and Leakey almost *never* had to balance the credibility of one piece of evidence against that of another. With only one exception, all evidence supported just one interpretation. I suggest that one need weigh the evidence for conflicting hypotheses only very rarely, because if a state of the world is consistent, then it will provide inconsistent signals relatively rarely.

These considerations suggest that weighing evidence may be one of the least useful approaches to resolving conflicting hypotheses. It is, after all, a decision to commit oneself to one hypothesis or the other on the basis of available evidence. But if the world is consistent, then conflicts can arise only because of incomplete knowledge of the world, and it seems that the right tack is not to choose the hypothesis with marginally better certainty, but to get some more evidence. It must be said, however, that if more evidence is simply not available, and there is no anticipation that it will become available in a useful time-frame, and a choice must be made between hypotheses, then ranking of bodies of endorsements must provide a basis for the choice. Even when it is not *necessary* to make a choice, it may be *desirable* to resolve one´s uncertainty by choosing the best endorsed alternative. This is especially true if the alternatives are numerous. It has been pointed out that the resolution and discounting methods discussed above are useful for small numbers of alternatives, and do not scale up very well.[2] In sum, it seems that weighing evidence to resolve conflicts may be necessary, or desirable, but it is not the obvious method to use; indeed, it may be less useful than numerous least commitment approaches, such as hedging, worst-case analysis, taking a central value,

[2] I thank Professor Shortliffe for this observation.

deciding not to decide, and so on.

Summary. The three general functions under discussion are building resolution tasks, propagating endorsements over inferences, and ranking endorsements. The first two require development, but I have suggested that the third function -- to decide which of two propositions is most certain -- is not obviously necessary. This is a fortuitous and unexpected outcome: At the beginning of the SOLOMON project I spent much time thinking about how to rank arbitrary collections of endorsements. I was having little success, so I built SOLOMON to run with very crude ranking criteria. I found that these suffice for the purpose of ranking tasks by their endorsements on SOLOMON's agenda, but I do not know whether the simple ranking algorithm developed for this purpose can be used for other cases where bodies of endorsements need ranking, such as choosing among conflicting conclusions. I think the algorithm is probably too weak, and that much remains to be learned about ranking bodies of endorsements. I adopted a similar simplifying tactic for the problem of propagation criteria, but with less success: The default rule for propagating endorsements results in long, messy lists of endorsements. Developments of new propagating rules, and of new resolution methods awaits scaling SOLOMON up to tasks that require more reasoning than is found in the FOLIO testbed.

5.4 Evaluating Model of Endorsement and SOLOMON

Chapter 3 compared the model of endorsement and Bayesian inference on purely utilitarian grounds -- as tools for expressing uncertain situations. I believe that this is the right approach to evaluating the model and SOLOMON. The program is intended for building expert systems. It will be like EMYCIN, but will provide the ability to reason about uncertainty and evidence. Some evaluation criteria for the model of endorsement and SOLOMON concern the ease of representing uncertain information; other criteria relate to the performance of systems developed in the SOLOMON framework. These are discussed in order.

Some questions one might ask about the representational adequacy of the model of endorsement are:

1. What aspects of uncertainty does the endorsement-based approach represent especially well or poorly?

2. Can one represent all pertinent aspects of uncertainty?

3. What kinds of tasks are especially amenable to the endorsement-based approach, and for which tasks is it a poor tool?

4. How much expertise is needed to use the the endorsement-based approach; is it too cumbersome or complicated to be useful?

5. Does the approach make unrealistic assumptions about the accuracy or availability of the evidence it requires from users?

In an attempt to model reasoning about uncertainty entirely with endorsements, without any reliance on opaque numerical degrees of belief, SOLOMON lost the power to easily make some comparative statements about hypotheses, such as, "I believe hypothesis 2 more than hypothesis 3." No tenet of the model of endorsement precludes using numerical degrees of belief, but it was decided that SOLOMON should use only symbolic endorsements. Comparisons between hypotheses are difficult in the model of endorsement because the model seeks to replace "net belief" with component reasons for believing. Thus, aggregate measures of belief that are easily ranked must, by design, be reduced to bodies of endorsements that are not easily ranked. It is quite possible that future implementations of SOLOMON will employ both numerical degrees of belief and endorsements -- reasons for belief. The advantages and disadvantages of both are discussed throughout this section.

Although it is difficult to make some comparisons between hypotheses, an advantage of the endorsement-based approach is that comparisons of endorsements are principled: There must be a rule somewhere in the system saying that one endorsement, or body of endorsements, is preferred to another. This solves the problem of meaningless comparisons of evidence. An infinite number of points exists between two degrees of belief, and they cannot *all* correspond to meaningful comparisons of hypotheses. We agree that if P(A) = .9 and P(B) = .2 then the former is more certain than the latter. But if P(B) = .87 the comparison may be meaningless. Decision analysts and statisticians recognize that all comparisons between arbitrary numbers are not meaningful, and they have developed sensitivity analysis and hypothesis testing techniques to determine what is a *significant difference*. In the model of endorsement, these elegant mathematical approaches are replaced by heuristic comparison criteria: A **corroboration** endorsement is preferred to a **contradiction** endorsement, a **cwa-not** endorsement is preferred to an **ostrich-not** endorsement.

Some aspects of the endorsement-based approach are cumbersome compared with the elegant numerical approaches, but endorsements have one major advantage over numbers: They contain *explicit* information about why one believes and disbelieves. Consequently, one can *reflect* on these records to decide how to act. The previous section outlined half a dozen resolutions that might apply to a conflict of values, such as averaging, hedging, worst-case analysis, and ignoring the discrepancy. It is obvious that these methods are not equally applicable to all kinds of conflicts, and just as obvious that one cannot choose an applicable method based on the degrees of belief of the conflicting hypotheses. An explicit record of the *kind* of conflict is needed.

These considerations suggest that the endorsement-based approach might be inappropriate for domains in which numerical degrees of belief have a clear semantics and are adequate representations of all the information about uncertainty that one might want to express, simply because the calculi of Bayesian inference or belief functions are very much less cumbersome than that of the model of endorsement. If we are satisfied that all degrees of belief have a common interpretation, such as a mixture of utility and probability arguments; and/or we do not care to separate these conceptual components of degrees of belief; and we are satisfied that our representation of uncertainty has the passive role of measuring how much we believe, instead of an active part in reducing, or at least discounting, uncertainty; and we do not need explanations of why we believe and disbelieve hypotheses; then the numerical approach to uncertainty might be preferable. Moreover, if we demand a normative calculus to ensure rational decisions, then we will prefer some numerical methods to the model of endorsement, at least for the process of assessment and combining of evidence. On the other hand, if we think that numerical degrees of belief mask distinctions that could be profitably used to reason about uncertainty, if we wish to regard kinds of uncertainty as problems to be solved by resolution or discounting methods, if we doubt that the requirements of normative approaches are met, and acknowledge that numerical methods are at best heuristic anyway, then the model of endorsement stands as an interesting and potentially powerful tool.

These arguments are all prospective; they say what you can *expect* to get for your efforts if you use an endorsement-based approach. They are backed-up by the prototype SOLOMON system. It is worth considering, also in prospect, how one might *prove* the utility of the SOLOMON approach. Some important criteria are the following performance tests:

1. Does the system give the "right answer" to problems of uncertainty? Is it ever convinced by unconvincing evidence, or skeptical of compelling evidence; and if so, is it easy to modify this inadequate performance?

2. Is the system blind to simple and intuitive resolutions of uncertainty? Is its reasoning about resolutions more complicated than necessary? For example, does it search high and low for corroboration when a simple request for more information would suffice?

3. Does reasoning about control make the system more efficient? Simple cases suggest that it does; for example, it obviously helps to screen out tasks that add nothing to SOLOMON´s certainty, tasks with redundant conclusions. It should be very easy to check the effect of the model of endorsement on the number of *domain inferences* that SOLOMON makes; more difficult is the question of whether reasoning about uncertainty is worth the effort.

4. Are there undesirable side-effects of the kind of reasoning that SOLOMON does. For example, we know that assumptions lead to nonmonotonic inferences (McDermott and Doyle, 1980), and that it is difficult to guarantee the consistency of a database under these circumstances. We know also that a powerful method for resolving uncertainty is assumption. Does its use lead to unacceptable consequences? If so, which characteristics of a domain disqualify assumption as a method?

A third factor that will facilitate evaluation of the model of endorsement is finding a domain in which its powers can be exercised. I have already noted that the asset-allocation problem of the FOLIO system is not especially taxing. A characteristic that one would desire in a domain is numerous *kinds* of uncertainy, such as uncertainty about the future, conflicting conclusions, noisy data, and a range of utilities for being right and wrong in uncertain choices. Much of the power of the model of endorsement derives from recognizing different kinds of uncertainty and resolving them in appropriate ways.

Evaluation of the model will be easier if the task domain has a hit rate. One of the problems with portfolio management is in evaluating whether reasoning about uncertainty improved the overall performance of the system, since "good" performance in portfolio management is open to interpretation. It is not necessarily the case that high-yield portfolios, or portfolios that closely match those of an invesment counselor, are good portfolios. Domains with signal understanding problems are probably a good source of tasks.

When I started work on the model of endorsement I intended it as a model of human reasoning about uncertainty. Demonstrating psychological validity has been tabled pending development of the model, but it is an evaluation criterion for the future. Currently, I can only claim that the approach is intuitive, and that it satisfies me as a model of my own introspections about reasoning about uncertainty. I am not so naive as to suggest this is adequate. I only suggest that the plausibibility of the approach encourages me to obtain hard psychological evidence. Some aspects of the model, I am convinced, will not progress without psychological evidence; for example, I have no idea whether rankings of endorsements are made on the basis of a few general criteria or a myriad of specific, pairwise rankings. Nor do I know how endorsements are dropped from inferences. I cannot believe that humans maintain *all* information pertinent to their belief -- all reasons for believing and disbelieving -- but I am ignorant of the principles that account for lost endorsements.

Finally, it is my goal that SOLOMON should function as an EMYCIN-like system for problems that involve reasoning about uncertainty. That is, I intend SOLOMON as a tool for building rule-based inference systems. Some things have been done to facilitate this goal; for example, the control structure and some knowledge representation conventions are consonant with current systems. Much remains to be done, however, especially in the area of knowledge representation. A rule-editor would be very helpful, especially if it incorporated meta-knowledge about the structure and function of endorsements. An explanation subsystem is essential, and as suggested by section 3.5, the explanations could be very illuminating by merit of information-rich endorsements. The future will tell whether the SOLOMON approach is indeed adequate to the task of sophisticated reasoning about uncertainty in a range of expert domains.

5.5 What the Future Really Holds

This section postdates the rest of this document by 10 months. It is intended as an addendum to bring the reader up to date on my research.[3] One focus of the research -- the issue to which we have devoted most attention -- is the problem of combining endorsements. (In earlier sections I distinguished between combining and propagating endorsements, but this distinction has proved unimportant in the last few months.) We have come to realize that the problem of combining endorsements cannot be solved convincingly unless we know what endorsements mean, and so we have been working on the semantics for the endorsements for a single, fairly general, problem domain. We also recognize that *any* combining mechanism must preserve the semantics of its domain: Just as modus ponens ensures that combinations of theorems will produce appropriate truth values, and Bayes´ theorem ensures that combinations of statements of probability will produce appropriate probabilities, so must combinations of endorsements produce appropriate endorsements. The key word in this observation is "appropriate"; what criteria determine whether a combination of truth values, probabilities, or endorsements is appropriate? In logic, combinations must be truth-preserving to ensure that inconsistent theorems are not deduced from consistent ones. For Bayes´ theorem, the derived numbers must satisfy the criteria of being probabilities. Modus ponens and Bayes´ theorem are thus combination rules that preserve the meaning of their domain. We have an identical requirement for rules to combine endorsements, as we shall illustrate shortly.

Combining evidence is something that numerical approaches to uncertainty do very well, because they represent uncertainty as a quantity increased or diminished

[3] I have had the good fortune to work with some excellent colleagues on the problems I discuss here. I gratefully acknowledge the contributions of Norman Carver, David Day, Alvah Davis, Brian Delaney, Tom Gruber, Philip Johnson, Larry Lefkowitz, Melinda Mesick, and Mike Sullivan.

by evidence. We do not represent uncertainty as a quantity: We represent it in terms of knowledge about evidence, and we do not summarize this knowledge in a degree of belief. Thus, it is not as easy to combine evidence in the theory of endorsements as it is in quantitative theories. If there is evidence from more than one source for a proposition, we must "calculate" a body of endorsements for the proposition by combining the endorsements of each piece of evidence. Simple syntactic union of the endorsements leads to the problems mentioned above: Large bodies of endorsements result, and not all endorsements remain relevant for all uses of their associated propositions. We are exploring *semantic combining rules* for endorsements -- so called because the combination of endorsements is mediated by rules that reflect what the endorsements mean.

The domain in which we are exploring issues of combining endorsements is plan recognition. In this task, a person types instructions to accomplish plan steps, and we try to determine which of several known plans the person has in mind, given knowledge about the plans and about the person. (A more sophisticated plan recognition system, called POISE, is the model for the the tasks we describe here. It is discussed in Carver, Lesser, and McCue, 1984.) Plan recognition is uncertain because an instruction may suggest more than one plan, and it may be a mistake. For example, imagine only two simple plans, each composed of just three steps:

plan 1: a b c
plan 2: b d e

If the first input is **a**, this results in a strong reason to believe that the most likely explanation (MLE) of **a** is plan 1, namely, there is no other explanation of **a**. Note, however, that **a** might have been a mistake. The endorsements of the statement MLE(**a**, plan1) are thus

MLE(**a**, plan 1)
1. no other explanation of **a** -- positive
2. **a** may be a mistake -- negative.

The next input is **b**. A possible explanation (PE)[4] is that **b** starts plan 2. However, our system knows some rudimentary facts about people that it uses as endorsements of interpretations of user actions. One such fact is that people prefer to do one thing at a time. This is an argument against the plan 2 explanation of **b**, because plan 1 is already believed to be underway. Note that the same fact is used as a *positive* endorsement of the plan 1 explanation of **b**:

PE(**b**, plan 1)
1. people prefer to do one thing at a time -- positive
2. there is another explanation of **b** -- negative
3. **b** may be a mistake -- negative

PE(**b**, plan 2)
1. people prefer to do one thing at a time -- negative
2. there is another explanation of **b** -- negative
3. **b** may be a mistake -- negative

Since **b** can continue plan 1, it is *further evidence* that the user has plan 1 in mind. We now consider how to combine the endorsements of plan 1 thus far, with the endorsements of the plan 1 explanation of **b**. The former endorsements are

MLE(**a**, plan 1)
1. no other explanation of **a** -- positive
2. **a** may be a mistake -- negative.

We invoke a *semantic combining rule*:

SCR-1: If an explanation of a step is negatively
endorsed by "may be a mistake," and
the successor of the step is the next input
Then drop the endorsement.

---

[4] We use the predicate PE, instead of MLE, to indicate that we haven´t yet decided which is the most likely explanation of the input.

In other words, since we got **b** immediately after **a**, we no longer believe that **a** could have been a mistake. The endorsements of plan 1 are thus

plan 1
1. no other explanation of **a** – positive
2. people prefer to do one thing at a time – positive
3. there is another explanation of **b** – negative
4. **b** may be a mistake – negative

Consider what happens if the next input is **d**. Now it appears that plan 1 has been suspended or was never intended (i.e., **a** was a mistake). Since **d** supports the interpretation that the user intends plan 2, we must ask how the endorsements of the plan 2 interpretation of **b** combine with the endorsements of **d**. These endorsements are:

PE(**b**, plan 2)
1. people prefer to do one thing at a time – negative
2. there is another explanation of **b** – negative
3. **b** may be a mistake – negative

MLE(**d**, plan 2)
1. no other explanation of **d** – positive
2. people prefer to do one thing at a time – positive
3. **d** may be a mistake – negative

To combine these endorsements we invoke SCR-1 to eliminate the concern that **b** might be a mistake. We also use a similar rule to eliminate the "people prefer to do one thing at a time" endorsement:

SCR-2: If an explanation of a step is negatively endorsed
by "people prefer to do one thing at a time," and
the successor of the step is the next input
Then drop the endorsement.

That is, we may have disbelieved that **b** started plan 2, since plan 1 was already open and people prefer to do one thing at a time. But since **d** continues plan 2, we believe that plan 2 was the intent of **b**, and the negative endorsement is erased. Thus, the combined endorsement of plan 2 is:

plan 2
1. there is another explanation of **b** -- negative
2. no other explanation of **d** -- positive
3. people prefer to do one thing at a time -- positive
4. **d** may be a mistake -- negative

We have not yet considered how an input such as **d** could constitute evidence against the interpretation that the user intends plan 1. Evidence for one plan is, in this domain, evidence against another, but we are eager to see whether endorsements of opposing interpretations can be combined. This is for the all-important reason that we want to reason about evidence in domains where the hypotheses are not necessarily mutually exclusive and exhaustive. Consider this example of how such reasoning might proceed: One of the positive endorsements of plan 1 is that people prefer to do one thing at a time; this results from the interpretation of **b** as following **a** in plan 1. But if plan 2 is, in fact, the intended plan, then **b** was intended as part of it, and the positive endorsement just mentioned is invalid. Thus, the strength of the positive endorsement depends on how much we believe plan 2 was intended. And so, the endorsement of plan 1 *can* be changed, but only by combination with the endorsements of the competing interpretation. It is this condition -- that of including endorsements of competing interpretations -- that makes calculating the *negative* import of evidence more complicated that calculating its positive impact.

Finally, we note that semantic combining rules that drop endorsements will occasionally produce curious bodies of endorsements. SCR-1 dropped the possibility that **a** was a mistake, which, if it still existed, we could use as further support for the plan 2 interpretation of the user´s actions. We could "tune" the combining rules to avoid this kind of situation, but we prefer not to: Our goal is a plausible theory of heuristic reasoning about uncertainty, and so we are just as interested in plausible errors as other behaviors.

Let us summarize this example, reiterating the theoretically interesting parts: The first thing to note is that the domain is plan recognition, and that a central concern is determining the user´s *intent*. Thus, some of the endorsements for the domain deal with intents. Among these is the **may-be-mistaken** endorsement. The meaning of this endorsement -- the way we interpret it -- is that an action that **may-be-mistaken** is one that is not consonant with the user´s intent. We can think of this as an axiom: Mistakes are unintended actions. We can develop other axioms of intent, for example, *Two consistent actions prove some intent*. We don´t always know *which* plan a user intends by two consistent actions (consider the plans **a b c**, **a b d**, and the consistent actions **a b**), but we *can* reasonably conclude that *some* intent is there, and, thus, that the actions are not mistakes. It is therefore legitimate to eliminate the endorsement **may-be-mistaken** in the light of consistent actions.

In sum, we proceed by first identifying the meaningful constructs (such as intent and mistake) in a domain. We then determine which of those constructs figure in assessing our certainty (e.g., the possibility of mistakes results in uncertainty), and state the influence of the construct on our certainty in either a positive or a negative endorsement. We then consider relationships among the constructs (e.g., a mistake is anything that is not intended). From these relationships we construct semantic combining rules (e.g., since a mistake is anything unintended, then proving an intent eliminates the suspicion of a mistake.) It is our goal now to develop a satisfactorily large number of axioms about intent and other constructs relevant to plan perception, and to follow the path we describe to derive a rich set of semantic combining rules. The fundamental insight here is that semantic combining rules prescribe the semantics of endorsements -- that is, the meaning of endorsements is how they combine with other endorsements. This guarantees that semantic combining rules preserve the meaning of endorsements, a guarantee that is almost always lacking for probabilistic rules for combining numbers that may or may not be probabilities.

6 References

Adams, J. B. 1976. A probability model of medical reasoning and the MYCIN model. *MATHEMATICAL BIOSCIENCES* **32**, 177-186.

Barr, A. B., and Feigenbaum, E. A. (Eds.) 1981. *The handbook of artificial intelligence, Volume I*. Los Altos, CA.: William Kaufmann, Inc.

Barr, A. B., and Feigenbaum, E. A. (Eds.) 1982. *The handbook of artificial intelligence, Volume II*. Los Altos, CA.: William Kaufmann, Inc.

Buchanan, B. G., and Duda, R. O. 1982. Principles of rule-based expert systems. Report No. STAN-CS-82-926. Stanford University.

Buchanan, B. G., and Shortliffe, E. H. 1984. *Rule-based expert systems: The MYCIN experiments of the Stanford Heuristic Programming Project*. Reading, Mass.: Addison-Wesley. In press.

Charniak, E., Riesbeck, C. K., and McDermott, D. V. 1980. *Artificial intelligence programming*. Hillsdale, N.J.: Lawrence Erlbaum Associates.

Cohen, H. 1979. What is an image. Proceedings of the sixth IJCAI. 1028-1057.

Cohen, P. R., and Feigenbaum, E. A. (Eds.) 1982. *The handbook of artificial intelligence, Volume III*. Los Altos, CA.: William Kaufmann, Inc.

Cohen, P. R., and Grinberg, M. R. 1983. A theory of heuristic reasoning about uncertainty. The AI Magazine. Summer, 1983.

Cohen, P. R., and Lieberman, M. D. 1983. FOLIO: An expert assistant for portfolio managers. *IJCAI 8*

Collins, A. M. 1978. Fragments of a theory of human plausible reasoning. TINLAP-2. 194-201.

Coombs, C. H., Dawes, R. M., and Tversky, A. 1970. *Mathematical psychology: An elementary introduction*. Prentice-Hall.

Davis, R. 1976. Applications of meta level knowledge to the construction, maintenance, and use of large knowledge bases. Rep. No. STAN-CS-76-564, Computer Science Department, Stanford University. (Doctoral dissertation.

Reprinted in R. Davis and D. B. Lenat (Eds.). 1980. *Knowledge based systems in artificial intelligence*. New York: McGraw-Hill.)

Davis, R. 1979. Panel on dealing with uncertainty. *6th IJCAI* pp. 1101-1102.

Dietterich, T. G. 1982. Learning. In P. R. Cohen and E. A. Feigenbaum (Eds.) *The handbook of artificial intelligence, Volume III*. Los Altos, CA.: William Kaufmann, Inc. 323-513

Doyle, J. 1979. A truth maintenance system. *Artificial Intelligence* 12:231-272.

Doyle, J. 1982. Nonmonotonic logics. In P. R. Cohen and E. A. Feigenbaum (Eds.) *The handbook of artificial intelligence, Volume III*. Los Altos, CA.: William Kaufmann, Inc. 114-119

Doyle, J. 1983. Reasoned assumptions. The AI Magazine. Summer, 1983.

Duda, R. O., Hart, P. E., and Nilsson, N. 1976. Subjective Bayesian methods for rule-based inference systems. Technical Note 124, Artificial Intelligence Center, SRI International, Menlo Park, CA.

Duda, R. O., Gaschnig, J., and Hart, P. 1979. Model design in the Prospector consultant system for mineral exploration. In D. Michie (Ed.) *Expert systems in the microelectronic age*, Edinburgh: Edinburgh University Press. 153-167.

Eddy, D. M. 1982. Probabilistic reasoning in clinical medicine: Problems and opportunities. In D. Kahneman, P. Slovic, and A. Tversky (Eds.) *Judgment under uncertainty: Heuristics and biases*. Cambridge: Cambridge University Press

Edwards, W. 1968. Conservatism in human information processing. In B. Kleinmuntz (Ed.), *Formal representation of human judgment*. New York: Wiley.

Engelmore, R. E., and Terry, A. 1979. Structure and function of the CRYSALIS system. *IJCAI 6*, 250-256.

Erman, L. D., Hayes-Roth, F., Lesser, V. R., and Reddy, D. R. 1980. The Hearsay speech understanding system: Integrating knowledge to resolve uncertainty. Computing Surveys 12:2.

Erman, L. D., and Lesser, V. R. 1975. A multi-level organization for problem solving using many diverse, coppoerating sources of knowledge. *IJCAI 4*, pp. 483-490.

Fikes, R. E., Hart, P. E., and Nilsson, N. J. 1972. Learning and executing generalized robot plans. *Artificial Intelligence* 3: 251-288

Gaines, B. R. 1976. Foundations of fuzzy reasoning. *Int. J. Man-Machine Studies*, **8**, 623-668.

Gardner, A.v.d.L. 1983. The design of a legal analysis program. Proceedings, National Conference on Artificial Intelligence. Forthcoming.

Genesereth, M. R. and Smith, D. E. 1982. Meta-Level Architecture. HPP Report 81-6. Department of Computer Science. Stanford University. Stanford, CA.

Gordon, J., and Shortliffe, E. H. 1983. The Dempster-Shafer theory of evidence and its relevance to expert systems. In Buchanan and Shortliffe, 1984.

Green, C. C. 1969. The application of theorem-proving to question-answering systems. *IJCAI I*, 219-237

Hanson, A. R., and Riseman, E. M. 1978. VISIONS: A computer system for interpreting scenes. In *Computer vision systems*, A. R. Hanson and E. M. Riseman (Eds.) New York: Academic Press. 303-333.

Hayes-Roth, B. and Hayes-Roth, F. 1979. A cognitive model of planning. *Cognitive Science* 3:275-310.

Hayes-Roth, B. 1983. Talk given at Stanford University.

Hayes-Roth, F., and Lesser, V. R. 1977. Focus of attention in the HEARSAY-II speech understanding system. Technical Report, no accession number. Carnegie-Mellon University, Pittsburgh, PA.

Hewitt, C. 1971. *Description and theoretical analysis (using schemas) of PLANNER: A language for proving theorems and manipulating models in a robot*. Doctoral dissertation. AI Laboratory. Massachusetts Institute of Technology.

Hillier, F. S., and Lieberman, G. J. 1980. Introduction to Operations Research. San Francisco, CA.: Holden-Day, Inc.

Kahneman, D. and Tversky, A. 1979. Prospect theory: An analysis of decisions under risk. *Econometrica, 47*, 263-291.

Kahneman, D., Slovic, P. and Tversky, A. 1982. *Judgements under uncertainty: Heuristics and biases*. Cambridge University Press.

Kanade, T., and Shafer, S. 1982. Vision. In P. Cohen and E. A., Feigenbaum (Eds.) *The handbook of artificial intelligence*. Los Altos, CA.: William Kaufmann, Inc. pp. 125-322.

Kornfeld, W. A., and Hewitt, C. E. 1981. The scientific community metaphor. *IEEE Transactions on Systems, Man, and Cybernetics,* **SMC-11:1** 24-33.

Langley, P. W. 1980. Descriptive discovery processes: Experiments in Baconian science. Rep. No. CS-80-121. Computer Science Department, Carnegie -Mellon University. (Doctoral dissertation)

Lea, W. (Ed.) 1980. *Trends in speech recognition*. Englewood Cliffs, N.J.: Prentice Hall.

Le Faivre, R. A. 1977. FUZZY reference manual. Computer Science Department, Rutgers University.

Lenat, D. B. 1976. AM: An artificial intelligence approach to discovery in mathematics as heuristic search. Rep. No. STAN-CS-76-570, Computer Science Department, Stanford University. (Doctoral dissertation).

Loftus, E. F. 1979. *Eyewitness testimony*. Cambridge, Mass.: Harvard University Press.

March, J. 1978. Bounded rationality, ambiguity, and the engineering of choice. *Bell Journal of Economics*, **9**, 587-608.

McCarthy, J. 1968. Programs with common sense. In M. L. Minsky (Ed.) *Semantic information processing*. Cambridge, Mass.: MIT Press, 403-409. Originally published in 1958.

McCarthy, J. and Hayes, P. J. 1969. Some philosophical problems from the standpoint of artificial intelligence. In D. Michie and B. Meltzer (Eds.) *Machine Intelligence 4*. Edinburgh: Edinburgh University Press, 463-502.

McCarthy, J. 1980. Circumscription -- A form of non-monotonic reasoning. *Artificial Intelligence* **13** 27-39.

McDermott, D. and Doyle, J. 1980. Non-monotonic logic I. *Artificial Intelligence* **13**, 41-72.

Meehl, P. E. 1954. *Clinical versus statistical prediction: A theoretical analysis and review of the evidence*. Minneapolis: University of Minnesota Press.

Michalski, R. S., Carbonell, J. G., and Mitchell, T. M. 1983. *Machine learning: An artificial intelligence approach.* Palo Alto, CA.: Tioga.

Minsky, M. 1975. A framework for representing knowledge. In P. Winston. (Ed.), *The psychology of computer vision.* New York: McGraw-Hill, 211-277.

Nii, H. P., and Aiello, N. 1979. AGE (Attempt to Generalize): A knowledge-based program for building knowledge-based programs. *IJCAI 6*, 645-655.

Nii, H. P. and Feigenbaum, E. A. 1978. Rule-based understanding of signals. In D. A. Waterman and F. Hayes-Roth (Eds.) *Pattern-directed inference systems.* New York: Academic Press. 483-501.

Nilsson, N. J. 1971. *Problem solving methods in artificial intelligence.* New York: McGraw-Hill.

Nilsson, N. J. 1980. *Principles of artificial intelligence.* Palo Alto, Calif.: Tioga.

Quinlan, J. R. 1982. INFERNO: A cautious approach to uncertain inference. RAND Note N-1898-RC, RAND Corporation, Santa Monica, CA.

Reiter, R. 1980. A logic for default reasoning. *Artificial Intelligence*, **13** 81-132

Rudd, A. and Clasing, H. J. 1982. Modern Portfolio Theory. Homewood, Illinois: Dow Jones-Irwin.

Rumelhart, D. 1976. Towards an interactive model of reading. Tech. Rep. 56, Center for Human Information Processing, University of California, San Diego.

Sacerdoti, E. D. 1977. A structure for plans and behavior. New York: American Elsevier. (Originally published in 1975)

Schlaifer, R. 1969. *Analysis of decisions under uncertainty.* New York: McGraw-Hill.

Shafer, G. 1976. *A mathematical theory of evidence.* Princeton, NJ.: Princeton University Press.

Shafer, G. and Tversky, A. 1983. Weighing evidence: The design and comparison of probability thought experiments. Under review.

Sharpe, W. F. 1970. Portfolio theory and capital markets. New York: McGraw-Hill

Sharpe, W. F. 1981. Investments. Englewood Cliffs, NJ.: Prentice-Hall.

Shirai, Y. 1973. A context sensitive line finder for recognition of polyhedra. *Artificial Intelligence* **4**, 95-119

Shortliffe, E. H. 1974. MYCIN: A rule-based computer program for advising physicians regarding antimicrobial therapy selection. Stanford University: STAN-CS-74-465.

Shortliffe, E. H., and Buchanan, B. G. 1975. A model of inexact reasoning in medicine. Mathematical Biosciences 23:351-379.

Shortliffe, E. H., Buchanan, B. G., and Feigenbaum, E. A. 1979. Knowledge engineering for medical decision making: A review of computer-based clinical decision aids. *Proceedings of the IEEE* **67**, **9**, 1207-1224.

Simon, H. A. 1957. *Models of man: Social and rational*. New York: Wiley.

Stallman, R. M., and Sussman, G. J. 1976. *Forward reasoning and dependency-directed backtracking in a system for computer-aided circuit analysis*. Memo 380. MIT Artificial Intelligence Laboratory.

Stefik, M. J. 1981. Planning with constraints. *Artificial Intelligence*, **16:2**, 111-140.

Sussman, G. J. 1975. A computer model of skill acquisition. New York: American Elsevier.

Szolovits, P. and Pauker, S. G. 1978. Categorical and Probabilistic Reasoning in Medical Diagnosis. *Artificial Intelligence* **11**, 115-144

Tenenbaum, J. M., and Barrow, H. G. 1976. IGS: A paradigm for integrating image segmentation and interpretations. *IJCPR 3*, 504-513.

Tversky, A. and Kahneman, D. 1971. Belief in the law of small numbers. *Psychological Bulletin*, **2**, 105-110.

Tversky, A. and Kahneman, D. 1974. Judgment under uncertainty: Heuristics and biases. *Science, 185*, 1124-1131.

Tversky, A. and Kahneman, D. 1981. The framing of decisions and the psychology of choice. *Science* **211**, 453-458

References

Van Melle, W. 1980. A domain-independent system that aids in constructing knowledge-based consultation programs. Report STAN-CS-80-820, Department of Computer Science, Stanford University.

Walker, A. and Leakey, R. E. F. 1978. The hominids of East Turkana. *Scientific American* August, 54-66.

Waltz, D. 1975. Generating semantic descriptions from drawings of scenes with shadows. In P. H. Winston (Ed.) *The psychology of computer vision.* New York: McGraw-Hill, 19-92.

Weiss, S. M., Kulikowski, C. A., Amarel, S., and Safir, A. 1978. A model-based method for computer-aided medical decision-making. *Artificial Intelligence* **11**:145-172

Winograd, T. 1980. Extended inference modes in reasoning. *Artificial Intelligence*, **13**, 5-26.

Wolf, J. and Woods, W. 1980. The HWIM speech understanding system. In Lea, *Trends*, 316-139.

Zadeh, L. A. 1965. Fuzzy sets. *Information and Control*, **8**, 338-353

Zadeh, L. A. 1978. Fuzzy sets as a basis for a theory of possibility. *Fuzzy Sets and Systems*, Amsterdam: North-Holland